Recent Advances in Integral Equations

Edited by Francisco Bulnes

Published in London, United Kingdom

IntechOpen

Supporting open minds since 2005

Recent Advances in Integral Equations
http://dx.doi.org/10.5772/intechopen.79094
Edited by Francisco Bulnes

Contributors
Francisco Bulnes, Nawab Hussain, Iram Iqbal, Isamu Doku, Weidong Chen, Naofumi Kitsunezaki

First published in London, United Kingdom, 2019 by IntechOpen
IntechOpen is the global imprint of INTECHOPEN LIMITED, registered in England and Wales, registration number: 11086078, The Shard, 25th floor, 32 London Bridge Street
London, SE19SG - United Kingdom
Printed in Croatia

British Library Cataloguing-in-Publication Data
A catalogue record for this book is available from the British Library

Additional hard and PDF copies can be obtained from orders@intechopen.com

Recent Advances in Integral Equations
Edited by Francisco Bulnes
p. cm.
Print ISBN 978-1-83880-658-3
Online ISBN 978-1-83880-657-6
eBook (PDF) ISBN 978-1-83880-659-0

Meet the editor

DR. FRANCISCO BULNES, PhD, PostDocs, Doctor H. C., HonDSc, zbMATH , PhD in Mathematical Sciences, IM/UNAM. IINAMEI Director, Mathematics Research Centre in Mexico, 2015-Actually. Editor-in-Chief of Journals of Mathematics, in USA, and India, 2015-Actually. Member of various international committees of science. Reviewer of British journals of mathematics and physics in SCOPUS; Head of Research Department, GI-TESCHA. Numerous papers (more than 100) in mathematics and physics research journals, and author of much books of mathematics and physics. Recognised and famous in East Europe, Asia, Arab continents. He has many theories, theorems, math objects with his name. He has received various honors by universities and NGO's, likewise GO's. Also is Czech Republic Mathematics Society distinguished member (JCFM). He has two post-doctorates in Cuba and Russia in mathematics. Many international awards and badges. www.iinamei.com.mx

Contents

Preface

Today, research into integral equations is fundamental to the increasing development of functional analysis, function theory, functional equations, and other areas in mathematics. Integral equations can solve problems of any nature in dynamical systems, partial differential equations, representation theory and its realizations through integral transforms, integration on infinite dimension spaces and their operators, algebra, inverse problems in control theory, and system analysis. This book includes five chapters written by prestigious experts and researchers who present their work on integral equations and related themes considering the wide content of concepts and methodologies. Some of these important aspects are the functional resolution of integral equations, operator theories to nonsymmetric and symmetric kernels, extension problems of Banach algebras to kernels of integral equations, and probabilistic methods to integral equations among others. The book has been divided into five sections to facilitate the search for research information.

Dr. Francisco Bulnes
Professor,
Research Department in Mathematics and Engineering,
TESCHA, Mexico IINAMEI,
Mexico

Section 1

Introduction

Chapter 1

Introductory Chapter: Frontier Research on Integral Equations and Recent Results

Francisco Bulnes

"Mathematics knows no races or geographic boundaries; for mathematics, the cultural world is one country"

- David Hilbert

1. General discussion

The themes of recent research are focused on nonlinear integral equations [1], the new numerical and adaptive methods of resolution of integral equations [2], the generalization of Fredholm integral equations [3] of second kind, integral equations in time scales and the spectral densities [3, 4], operator theories for nonsymmetric and symmetric kernels [1, 5], extension problems to Banach algebras to kernels of integral equations [5–7], singular integral equations [10], special treatments to solve Fredholm integral equations of first and second kinds, nondegenerate kernels [3, 6] and symbols of integral equations [7], topological methods for the resolution of integral equations and representation problems of operators of integral equations.

Now, well, the field of the integral equations is not finished yet, not much less with the integral equations for which the Fredholm theorem is worth [fredholm], nor with the completely continuous operators, since there exist other integral equations developed of the Hilbert theory respect to the Fredholm discussion, and studies on singular integral equations, also by Hilbert, Wiener and others [8]. Arise numerical and approximate methods on the big vastness that give the Banach algebras, even using probabilistic measures to solve some integral equations in the ambit of distributions and stochastic process. Likewise, there arise integral equations in which the proper values are corresponded to linearly independent infinite proper functions. Such is the case, for example, of the Lalesco-Picard integral equation:

$$\omega(t) - \lambda \int_{-\infty}^{+\infty} e^{-|t-s|}\omega(s)\mathrm{ds} = f(t), \tag{1}$$

in which the kernel $e^{-|t-s|}$ is not of L^2class and gives a continuous spectra, or even, we consider nonlinear integral equations, etc., that represent the last and recent studies on integral equations after of their study considering extensions of the Banach algebras to integral operators that can define to this proposit, for example, to singular integral equations.

Likewise, as special case, for their important theory, we can treat the singular integral equations of Cauchy. This theory was created almost immediately after the Fredholm theory, and their beginning is given in the "Lecons de Mécanique

Céleste" by Poincaré and Fichot [9], and to the Hilbert works on contour and boundary problems of the analytic functions theory.

A possible treatment, bringing the Cauchy ideas together with Banach algebras, is the consideration of the Calkin algebra $\frac{B(X)}{K(X)}$, on a Banach space X, likewise as the operators of subalgebras of this special Banach algebra (e.g., the algebra of the bounded operators $B(X)$, and $K(X)$, the ideal of compact operators) [10]. For example, consider the bounded operators in a Banach space with closed range and with kernel and co-kernel of finite dimension. These are called Fredholm operators and are the operators that give invertible elements of the Calkin algebra. The operators of the Calkin algebra radical are called Reisz operators and can be characterized spectrally and in terms of the dimensions of $\mathrm{Rec}\left((\lambda I - T)^k\right)$, $\ker\left((\lambda I - T)^k\right)$, etc. Very questions on these algebras are motive of modern research. However, also the integral equations research has developed more the functional analysis, considering the function theory, integral transforms and the Kernels study in a wide form.

For other side, a general resolution method to the singular integral equations cannot be given in detail on the effective resolution of these equations, because is followed the research on a general methods to this integral equations class through certain special functions and integral transforms, which are of diverse and varied nature [5, 11]. In fact, the resolution of singular integrals considering the Hilbert transform and the Fourier transform [11] has been in the last years strongly researched. Here we only consider the intimate relation between this singular integral equations theory with the analytic functions theory and special functions related with the regularity and completeness of the solutions required.

One of the new developments on nonlinear integral equations are followed to the Hammerstein integral equations [12], which is written as

$$\omega(t) + \int_a^b K(t,s)f(s,\omega(s))\mathrm{ds} = 0, \quad a \le t \le b \tag{2}$$

where $K(t,s)$ and $f(t,s)$ are given functions, while $\omega(t)$ is the unknown function. Hammerstein considered for $K(t,s)$, a symmetric and positive Fredholm kernel. This last condition establishes that all their eigenvalues are positive. Thus, the function $f(t,s)$ is continuous and satisfies $|f(t,s)| \le C_1|s| + C_2$, where C_1 and C_2 are positive constants and C_1 is smaller than the first eigenvalue of the kernel $K(t,s)$; then, the Hammerstein integral equation has at least one continuous solution. Also are considered certain observations on the no decreasing of the function $f(t,s)$, on s, considering fix t, from the interval (a,b).The Hammerstein's equation cannot have more than one solution. This property holds also if $f(t,s)$ satisfies the condition

$$|f(t,s_1) - f(t,s_2)| \le C|s_1 - s_2|, \tag{3}$$

where the positive constant C is smaller than the first eigenvalue of the kernel $K(t,s)$. A solution of the Hammerstein equation may be constructed by the method of successive approximation. In regard to this point, many approximation methods are designed to solve these integral equations and other nonlinear integral equations. Also of interest are the recent developments on Hammerstein-Volterra integral equations:

$$f(t) = \omega(t) + \int_0^t K(t,s)f(s,\omega(s))\mathrm{ds}, \qquad 0 \le t \le 1 \tag{4}$$

In the aspect of the linear integral equations has been important the study of the Volterra integral equations on time scale, where have more importance the initial value problems with unbounded domains. Likewise, the development on the alternate form of a linear integral equation is given as:

$$f(t) = \omega(t) + \int_a^t B(t,s)\omega^\sigma(s)\mathrm{d}s, \quad t \in I_T \tag{5}$$

where $B(t,s)$ is a kernel that comes of a Banach algebra, and ω^σ, arises naturally of changing dynamics problems, for example the economic dynamics. Some aspects in their prospective can be extended to the nonlinear case.

Other studies go on to develop generalizations of integral equations of Fredholm type using Weyl fractional integral operators and the kernel as product of certain generalized functions of special functions such as the H functions and the I functions. This establishes new techniques in function theory and functional analysis relating some integral transforms such as the Mellin transform [13].

Other developments start the probabilistic methods searching the obtaining of a solution of some integral equations of the second kind and Volterra integral equation, thinking in stochastic phenomena where is necessary determine an aleatory behavior.

Author details

Francisco Bulnes[1,2]

1 Research Department in Mathematics and Engineering, TESCHA, Mexico

2 IINAMEI, Mexico

*Address all correspondence to: francisco.bulnes@tesch.edu.mx

References

[1] Tricomi FC. Integral Equations. Interscience Publishers; 1957

[2] Arfken G. Neumann series, separable (degenerate) kernels. In: Mathematical Methods for Physicists. 3rd ed. Orlando, FL: Academic Press; 1985. pp. 879-890

[3] Ruston AF. Direct products of Banach spaces and linear functional equations. Proceedings of the London Mathematical Society. 1953;**1**(3):327-384

[4] Ruston AF. On the Fredholm theory of integral equations for operators belonging to the trace class of a general Banach space. Proceedings of the London Mathematical Society. 1951; **53**(2):109-124

[5] Kolmogorov AN, Fomin SV. Elementos de la Teoría de Funciones y del Análisis Funcional. URSS: Mir Moscú; 1975

[6] Polyanin AD, Manzhirov AV. Handbook of Integral Equations. Boca Raton: CRC Press; 1998

[7] Taylor M. Pseudo-Differential Operators (PMS-34). N.J, USA: Princeton University Press; 1981

[8] Muskhelishmili. Singular Integral Equations. New York, USA: Dover Publications; 2008

[9] Poincaré H, Fichot E. Lecons de Mécanique Céleste: Théorie Générale Des Perturbations Planétaires. Sydney, New South Wales: Wentworth Press; 1918

[10] Calkin JW. Two-sided ideals and congruences in the ring of bounded operators in Hilbert space. The Annals of Mathematics. 1941;**42**(4):839. DOI: 10.2307/1968771

[11] Titchmarsh EC. Theory of Fourier Integrals. Oxford: Oxford University Press; 1937

[12] Hammerstein A. Nichtlineare integralgleichungen nebst anwendungen. Acta Mathematica. 1930; **54**:117-176

[13] Chaurasia VBL, Singh Y. New generalization of integral equations of fredholm type using aleph-function. International Journal of Modern Mathematical Sciences. 2014;**9**(3):208-220

Section 2

Tools and Fundaments to Integral Equations and Their Solution Methods

Chapter 2

Contraction Mappings and Applications

Nawab Hussain and Iram Iqbal

Abstract

The aim of the chapter is to find the existence results for the solution of non-homogeneous Fredholm integral equations of the second kind and non-linear matrix equations by using the fixed point theorems. Here, we derive fixed point theorems for two different type of contractions. Firstly, we utilize the concept of manageable functions to define multivalued $\alpha_* - \eta_*$ manageable contractions and prove fixed point theorems for such contractions. After that, we use these fixed point results to find the solution of non-homogeneous Fredholm integral equations of the second kind. Secondly, we introduce weak $\mathcal{F}$ contractions named as α-$\mathcal{F}$-weak-contraction to prove fixed point results in the setting of metric spaces and by using these results we find the solution for non-linear matrix equations.

Keywords: contraction mapping, fixed point, integral equations, matrix equations, manageable function

1. Introduction

Let $H(n)$ denote the set of all $n \times n$ Hermitian matrices, $P(n)$ the set of all $n \times n$ Hermitian positive definite matrices, $S(n)$ the set of all $n \times n$ positive semidefinite matrices. Instead of $X \in P(n)$ we will write $X > 0$. Furthermore, $X \geq 0$ means $X \in S(n)$. Also we will use $X \geq Y$ $(X \leq Y)$ instead of $X - Y \geq 0 (Y - X \geq 0)$. The symbol $\|.\|$ denotes the spectral norm, that is,

$$\|A\| = \sqrt{\lambda^+(A^*A)},$$

where $\lambda^+(A^*A)$ is the largest eigenvalue of A^*A. We denote by $\|.\|_1$ the Ky Fan norm defined by

$$\|A\|_1 = \sum_{i=1}^{n} s_i(A),$$

where $s_i(A), i = 1, \ldots, n$, are the singular values of A. Also,

$$\|A\|_1 = tr\left((A^*A)^{1/2}\right),$$

which is $tr(A)$ for (Hermitian) nonnegative matrices. Then the set $H(n)$ endowed with this norm is a complete metric space. Moreover, $H(n)$ is a partially ordered set with partial order $\preccurlyeq$, where $X \preccurlyeq Y \Leftrightarrow Y \preccurlyeq X$. In this section, denote $d(X,Y) = \|Y - X\|_1 = tr(Y - X)$. Now, consider the non-linear matrix equation

$$X = Q + \sum_{i=1}^{m} A_i^* \gamma(X) A_i, \tag{1}$$

where Q is a positive definite matrix, $A_i, i = 1, \ldots, m$, are arbitrary $n \times n$ matrices and γ is a mapping from $H(n)$ to $H(n)$ which maps $P(n)$ into $P(n)$. Assume that γ is an order-preserving mapping (γ is order preserving if $A, B \in H(n)$ with $A \preccurlyeq B$ implies that $\gamma(A) \preccurlyeq \gamma(B)$). There are various kinds of problems in control theory, dynamical programming, ladder networks, etc., where the matrix equations plays a crucial role. Matrix Eq. (1) have been studied by many authors see [1–3].

At the same time, integral equations have been developed to solve boundary value problems for both ordinary and partial differential equations and play a very important role in nonlinear analysis. Many problems of mathematical physics, theory of elasticity, viscodynamics fluid and mixed problems of mechanics of continuous media reduce to the Fredholm integral Eq. A rich literature on existence of solutions for nonlinear integral equations, which contain particular cases of important integral and functional equations can be found, for example, see [4–14]. An important technique to solve integral equations is to construct an iterative procedure to generate approximate solutions and find their limit, a host of attractive methods have been proposed for the approximate solutions of Fredholm integral equations of the second kind, see [15–19]. We consider a non-homogeneous Fredholm integral equation of second kind of the form

$$z(r) = \int_b^c \mathcal{B}(r, s, z(s)) ds + g(r), \tag{2}$$

where $t \in [b, c]$, $\mathcal{B} : [b, c] \times [b, c] \times \mathbb{R}^n \to \mathbb{R}^n$ and $g : \mathbb{R}^n \to \mathbb{R}^n$.

An advancement in this direction is to find the solution of such mathematical models by using fixed point theorems. In this technique, we generate a sequence by iterative procedure for some self-map T and then look for a fixed point of T, that is actually the solution of given mathematical model. The simplest case is when T is a contraction mapping, that is a self-mapping satisfying

$$d(Tx, Ty) \leq kd(x, y),$$

where $k \in [0, 1)$. The contraction mapping principle [20] guarantees that a contraction mapping of a complete metric space to itself has a unique fixed point which may be obtained as the limit of an iteration scheme defined by repeated images under the mapping of an arbitrary starting point in the space. The multivalued version of contraction mapping principle can be found in [21]. In general, fixed point theorems allow us to obtain existence theorems concerning investigated functional-operator equations.

In this chapter, we prove the existence of solution for matrix Eq. (1) and integral Eq. (2) by using newly developed fixed point theorems.

2. Background material from fixed point theory

Let $\mathcal{X}$ be a set of points, a distance function on $\mathcal{X}$ is a map $d : \mathcal{X} \times \mathcal{X} \to [0, \infty)$ that is symmetric, and satisfies $d(i, i) = 0$ for all $i \in \mathcal{X}$. The distance is said to be a metric if the triangle inequality holds, i.e.,

$$d(i,j) \le d(i,k) + d(k,j),$$

for all $i, j, k \in \mathcal{X}$ and $(\mathcal{X}, d)$ is called metric space.

Denote by $2^{\mathcal{X}}$, the family of all nonempty subsets of $\mathcal{X}$, $CL(\mathcal{X})$, the family of all nonempty and closed subsets of $\mathcal{X}$, $CB(\mathcal{X})$, the family of all nonempty, closed, and bounded subsets of $\mathcal{X}$ and $K(\mathcal{X})$, the family of all nonempty compact subsets of $\mathcal{X}$. It is clear that, $K(\mathcal{X}) \subseteq CB(\mathcal{X}) \subseteq CL(\mathcal{X}) \subseteq 2^{\mathcal{X}}$, let

$$H(\mathcal{A}, \mathcal{B}) = \max\left\{ \sup_{x \in \mathcal{A}} D(x, \mathcal{B}), \sup_{y \in \mathcal{B}} D(y, \mathcal{A}) \right\},$$

where $D(x, \mathcal{B}) = \inf\{d(x,y) : y \in \mathcal{B}\}$. Then H is called generalized Pompeiu Hausdorff distance on $CL(\mathcal{X})$. It is well known that H is a metric on $CB(\mathcal{X})$, which is called Pompeiu Hausdorff metric induced by d.

If $\mathcal{T} : \mathcal{X} \to \mathcal{X}$ is a single valued self-mapping on $\mathcal{X}$, then $\mathcal{T}$ is said to have a fixed point x if $\mathcal{T}x = x$ and if $\mathcal{T} : \mathcal{X} \to 2^{\mathcal{X}}$ is multivalued mapping, then $\mathcal{T}$ is said to have a fixed point x if $x \in \mathcal{T}x$. We denote by $Fix\{\mathcal{T}\}$, the set of all fixed points of mapping $\mathcal{T}$.

Definition 2.1 [22] Let $\mathcal{T} : \mathcal{X} \to 2^{\mathcal{X}}$ be a multivalued map on a metric space $(\mathcal{X}, d)$, $\alpha, \eta : \mathcal{X} \times \mathcal{X} \to \mathbb{R}+$ be two functions where η is bounded, then $\mathcal{T}$ is an α_*-admissible mapping with respect to η, if

$$\alpha(y,z) \ge \eta(y,z) \text{ implies that } \alpha_*(\mathcal{T}y, \mathcal{T}z) \ge \eta_*(\mathcal{T}y, \mathcal{T}z), \quad y, z \in \mathcal{X},$$

where

$$\alpha_*(\mathcal{A}, \mathcal{B}) = \inf_{y \in \mathcal{A}, z \in \mathcal{B}} \alpha(y,z), \quad \eta_*(\mathcal{A}, \mathcal{B}) = \sup_{y \in \mathcal{A}, z \in \mathcal{B}} \eta(y,z).$$

Further, Definition 2.1 is generalized in the following way.

Definition 2.2 [23] Let $\mathcal{T} : \mathcal{X} \to 2^{\mathcal{X}}$ be a multivalued map on a metric space $(\mathcal{X}, d)$, $\alpha, \eta : \mathcal{X} \times \mathcal{X} \to [0, \infty)$ be two functions. We say that $\mathcal{T}$ is generalized α_*-admissible mapping with respect to η, if

$$\alpha(y,z) \ge \eta(y,z) \text{ implies that } \alpha(u,v) \ge \eta(u,v), \quad \text{for all } u \in \mathrm{T}y, v \in \mathrm{T}z.$$

If $\eta(y,z) = 1$ for all $y, z \in \mathcal{X}$, then $\mathcal{T}$ is said to be generalized α_*-admissible mapping.

3. Some fixed point results

Consistent with Du and Khojasteh [24], we denote by $\widehat{Man(\mathbb{R})}$, the set of all manageable functions $\vartheta : \mathbb{R} \times \mathbb{R} \to \mathbb{R}$ fulfilling the following conditions:

(ϑ_1) $\vartheta(t,s) < s - t$ for all $s, t > 0$;

(ϑ_2) for any bounded sequence $\{t_n\} \subset (0, +\infty)$ and any nondecreasing sequence $\{s_n\} \subset (0, +\infty)$, it holds that

$$\limsup_{n \to \infty} \frac{t_n + \vartheta(t_n, s_n)}{s_n} < 1. \tag{3}$$

Example 3.1 *[24] Let $r \in [0, 1)$. Then $\vartheta_r : \mathbb{R} \times \mathbb{R} \to \mathbb{R}$ defined by $\vartheta_r(t,s) = rs - t$ is a manageable function.*

Example 3.2 *Let* $\vartheta : \mathbb{R} \times \mathbb{R} \to \mathbb{R}$ *defined by*

$$\vartheta(t,s) = \begin{cases} \psi(s) - t & \text{if } (t,s) \in [0,+\infty) \times [0,+\infty), \\ f(t,s) & \textit{otherwise,} \end{cases}$$

where $\psi : [0,+\infty) \to [0,+\infty)$ satisfying $\sum_{n=1}^{\infty} \psi^n(t) < +\infty$ for all $t > 0$ and $f : \mathbb{R} \times \mathbb{R} \to \mathbb{R}$ is any function. Then $\vartheta(t,s) \in \widehat{Man(\mathbb{R})}$. Indeed, by using Lemma 1 of [25], we have for any $s, t > 0$, $\vartheta(t,s) = \psi(s) - t < s - t$, so, (ϑ_1) holds. Let $\{t_n\} \subset (0,+\infty)$ be a bounded sequence and let $\{s_n\} \subset (0,+\infty)$ be a nonincreasing sequence. Then $\lim_{n\to\infty} s_n = \inf_{n \in \mathbb{N} s_n} = a$ for some $a \in [0,+\infty)$, we get

$$\limsup_{n\to\infty} \frac{t_n + \vartheta(t_n, s_n)}{s_n} = \limsup_{n\to\infty} \frac{\psi(s_n)}{(s_n)} < \lim_{n\to\infty} \frac{(s_n)}{(s_n)} = 1,$$

so, (ϑ_2) is also satisfied.

Definition 3.3 Let $(\mathcal{X}, d)$ be a metric space and $T : \mathcal{X} \to 2^{\mathcal{X}}$ be a closed valued mapping. Let $\alpha, \eta : \mathcal{X} \times \mathcal{X} \to \mathbb{R}+$ be two functions and $\vartheta \in \widehat{Man(\mathbb{R})}$. Then T is called a multivalued $\alpha_* - \eta_*$-manageable contraction with respect to ϑ if for all $y, z \in \mathcal{X}$

$$\alpha_*(Ty, Tz) \geq \eta_*(Ty, Tz) \quad \text{implies} \quad \vartheta(H(Ty, Tz), d(y,z)) \geq 0. \tag{4}$$

Now we prove first result of this section.

Theorem 3.4 *Let* $(\mathcal{X}, d)$ *be a complete metric space and let* $T : \mathcal{X} \to 2^{\mathcal{X}}$ *be a closed valued map satisfying following conditions:*

1. T *is* α_**-admissible map with respect to* η*;*

2. T *is* $\alpha_* - \eta_*$ *manageable contraction with respect to* ϑ*;*

3. *there exists* $z_0 \in \mathcal{X}$ *and* $z_1 \in Tz_0$ *such that* $\alpha(z_0, z_1) \geq \eta(z_0, z_1)$*;*

4. *for a sequence* $\{z_n\} \subset \mathcal{X}$, $\lim_{n\to\infty}\{z_n\} = x$ *and* $\alpha(z_n, z_{n+1}) \geq \eta(z_n, z_{n+1})$ *for all* $n \in \mathbb{N}$*, implies* $\alpha(z_n, x) \geq \eta(z_n, x)$ *for all* $n \in \mathbb{N}$.

Then $Fix\{T\} \neq \emptyset$.

Proof. Let $z_1 \in Tz_0$ be such that $\alpha(z_0, z_1) \geq \eta(z_0, z_1)$. Since T is α_*-admissible map with respect to η, then $\alpha_*(Tz_0, Tz_1) \geq \eta_*(Tz_0, Tz_1)$. Therefore, from (4) we have

$$\vartheta(H(Tz_0, Tz_1), d(z_0, z_1)) \geq 0. \tag{5}$$

If $z_1 = z_0$, then $z_0 \in Fix\{T\}$, also if $z_1 \in Tz_1$, then $z_1 \in Fix\{T\}$. So, we adopt that $z_0 \neq z_1$ and $z_1 \notin Tz_1$. Thus $0 < d(z_1, Tz_1) \leq H(Tz_0, Tz_1)$. Define $\lambda : \mathbb{R} \times \mathbb{R} \to \mathbb{R}$ by

$$\lambda(t,s) = \begin{cases} \dfrac{t + \vartheta(t,s)}{s} & \text{if } t, s > 0 \\ 0 & \text{otherwise.} \end{cases} \tag{6}$$

By (ϑ_1), we know that

$$0 < \lambda(t,s) < 1 \qquad \text{for all } t, s > 0. \tag{7}$$

Also note that if $\vartheta(t,s) \geq 0$, then

$$0 < t \leq s\lambda(t,s). \tag{8}$$

So, from (5) and (7), we get

$$0 < \lambda(H(\mathcal{T}z_0, \mathcal{T}z_1), d(z_0,z_1)) < 1. \tag{9}$$

Let

$$\varepsilon_1 = \left(\frac{1}{\sqrt{\lambda(H(\mathcal{T}z_0, \mathcal{T}z_1), d(z_0,z_1))}} - 1\right) d(z_1, \mathcal{T}z_1). \tag{10}$$

Since $d(z_1, \mathcal{T}z_1) > 0$. So, by using (9), we get $\varepsilon_1 > 0$ and

$$\begin{aligned} d(z_1, \mathcal{T}z_1) &< d(z_1, \mathcal{T}z_1) + \varepsilon_1 \\ &= \left(\frac{1}{\sqrt{\lambda(H(\mathcal{T}z_0, \mathcal{T}z_1), d(z_0,z_1))}}\right) d(z_1, \mathcal{T}z_1). \end{aligned} \tag{11}$$

This implies that there exists $z_2 \in \mathcal{T}z_1$ such that

$$d(z_1,z_2) < \left(\frac{1}{\sqrt{\lambda(H(\mathcal{T}z_0, \mathcal{T}z_1), d(z_0,z_1))}}\right) d(z_1, \mathcal{T}z_1). \tag{12}$$

By induction, we form a sequence $\{z_n\}$ in $\mathcal{X}$ satisfying for each $n \in \mathbb{N}$, $z_n \in \mathcal{T}z_{n-1}$, $z_n \neq z_{n-1}$, $z_n \notin \mathcal{T}z_n$, $\alpha_*(z_{n-1},z_n) \geq \eta_*(z_{n-1},z_n)$,

$$0 < d(x_n, \mathcal{T}x_n) \leq H(\mathcal{T}z_{n-1}, \mathcal{T}z_n), \tag{13}$$

$$\vartheta(H(\mathcal{T}z_{n-1}, \mathcal{T}z_n), d(z_{n-1},z_n)) \geq 0, \tag{14}$$

and

$$d(z_n,z_{n+1}) < \left(\frac{1}{\sqrt{\lambda(H(\mathcal{T}z_{n-1}, \mathcal{T}z_n), d(z_{n-1},z_n))}}\right) d(z_n, \mathcal{T}z_n), \tag{15}$$

by taking

$$\varepsilon_n = \left(\frac{1}{\sqrt{\lambda(H(\mathcal{T}z_{n-1}, \mathcal{T}z_n), d(z_{n-1},z_n))}} - 1\right) d(z_n, \mathcal{T}z_n). \tag{16}$$

By using (7), (8), (13), and (15), we get for each $n \in \mathbb{N}$

$$d(z_n, \mathcal{T}z_n) \leq d(z_{n-1},z_n)\lambda(H(\mathcal{T}z_{n-1}, \mathcal{T}z_n), d(z_{n-1},z_n)) \leq d(z_{n-1},z_n), \tag{17}$$

this implies that $\{d(z_n, \mathcal{T}z_n)\}_{n \in \mathbb{N}}$ is a bounded sequence. By combining (15) and (17), for each $n \in \mathbb{N}$, we get

$$d(z_n,z_{n+1}) < \left(\sqrt{\lambda(H(\mathcal{T}z_{n-1}, \mathcal{T}z_n), d(z_{n-1},z_n))}\right) d(z_{n-1},z_n). \tag{18}$$

Which means that $\{d(z_{n-1},z_n)\}_{n \in \mathbb{N}}$ is a monotonically decreasing sequence of non-negative reals and so it must be convergent. So, let $\lim_{n\to\infty} d(z_n,z_{n+1}) = c \geq 0$. From (ϑ_2), we get

$$\lim_{n\to\infty} \sup\lambda(H(Tz_n, Tz_n), d(z_{n-1}, z_n)) < 1. \tag{19}$$

Now, if $c > 0$, then by taking the $\lim_{n\to\infty}$ sup in (18) and using (19), we have

$$c \leq \sqrt{\lim_{n\to\infty} \sup \lambda(H(Tz_{n-1}, Tz_n), d(z_{n-1}, z_n))c} < c. \tag{20}$$

This contradiction shows that $c = 0$. Hence, $\lim_{n\to\infty} d(z_n, z_{n+1}) = 0$. Next, we prove that $\{z_n\}_{n\in\mathbb{N}}$ is a Cauchy sequence in $\mathcal{X}$. Let, for each $n \in \mathbb{N}$,

$$\sigma_n = \sqrt{\lambda(H(Tz_{n-1}, Tz_n), d(z_{n-1}, z_n))}, \tag{21}$$

then from Eq. (9), we have $\sigma_n \in (0, 1)$. By (18), we obtain

$$d(z_n, z_{n+1}) < \sigma_n d(z_{n-1}, z_n). \tag{22}$$

(19) implies that $\lim_{n\to\infty} \sigma_n < 1$, so there exists $\gamma \in [0, 1)$ and $n_0 \in \mathbb{N}$, such that

$$\sigma_n \leq \gamma \quad \text{for all } n \in \mathbb{N}, n \geq n_0. \tag{23}$$

For any $n \geq n_0$, since $\sigma_n \in (0, 1)$ for all $n \in \mathbb{N}$ and $\gamma \in [0, 1)$, (22, 23) implies that

$$d(z_n, z_{n+1}) < \sigma_n d(z_{n-1}, z_n) < \sigma_n \sigma_{n-1} d(z_{n-2}, z_{n-1}) \cdots \leq \gamma^{n-n_0+1} d(z_0, z_1). \tag{24}$$

Put $\beta_n = \left(\frac{\gamma^{n-n_0+1}}{1-\gamma}\right) d(z_0, z_1)$, $n \in \mathbb{N}$. For $m, n \in \mathbb{N}$ with $m > n \geq n_0$, we have from (24) that

$$d(z_n, z_m) \leq \sum_{j=n}^{m-1} d(z_j, z_{j+1}) < \beta_n. \tag{25}$$

Since $\gamma \in [0, 1)$, $\lim_{n\to\infty}\beta_n = 0$. Hence $\lim_{n\to\infty}\sup\{d(z_n, z_m) : m > n\} = 0$. This shows that $\{z_n\}$ is a Cauchy sequence in $\mathcal{X}$. Completeness of $\mathcal{X}$ ensures the existence of $z \in \mathcal{X}$ such that $z_n \to z$ as $n \to \infty$. Now, since $\alpha(z_n, z) \geq \eta(z_n, z)$ for all $n \in \mathbb{N}$, $\alpha_*(Tz_n, Tz) \geq \eta_*(Tz_n, Tz)$, and so from (4), we have $\vartheta(H(Tz_n, Tz), d(z_n, z)) \geq 0$. Then from (7, 8), we have

$$H(Tz_n, Tz) \leq \lambda(H(Tz_n, Tz), d(z_n, z)) d(z_n, z) < d(z_n, z). \tag{26}$$

Since $0 < d(z, Tz) \leq H(Tz_n, Tz) + d(z_n, z)$, so by using (26), we get

$$0 < d(z, Tz) < 2d(z_n, z). \tag{27}$$

Letting limit $n \to \infty$ in above inequality, we get $d(z, Tz) = 0$. Hence $z \in Fix\{T\}$. □

Let $\Delta(F)$ be the set of all functions $\mathcal{F} : \mathbb{R}+ \to \mathbb{R}$ satisfying following conditions:

$(\mathcal{F}_1)$ $\mathcal{F}$ is strictly increasing;

$(\mathcal{F}_2)$ for all sequence $\{\alpha_n\} \subseteq R^+$, $\lim_{n\to\infty} \alpha_n = 0$ if and only if $\lim_{n\to\infty}\mathcal{F}(\alpha_n) = -\infty$;

$(\mathcal{F}_3)$ there exist $0 < k < 1$ such that $\lim_{n\to 0^+}\alpha^k \mathcal{F}(\alpha) = 0$,

$\Delta(F_*)$, if $\mathcal{F}$ also satisfies the following:

$(\mathcal{F}_4)$ $\mathcal{F}(\inf A) = \inf \mathcal{F}(A)$ for all $A \subset (0, \infty)$ with $\inf A > 0$,

Definition 3.5 [27] Let $(\mathcal{X}, d)$ be a metric space. A mapping $T : \mathcal{X} \to \mathcal{X}$ is said to be $\mathcal{F}$-contraction of there exists $\tau > 0$ such that

$$d(\mathcal{T}x, \mathcal{T}y) > 0 \quad \text{implies} \quad \tau + \mathcal{F}(d(\mathcal{T}x, \mathcal{T}y)) \leq \mathcal{F}(d(x,y)).$$

Theorem 3.6 *[26] Let $(\mathcal{X}, d)$ be a complete metric space and let $\mathcal{T} : \mathcal{X} \to \mathcal{X}$ be an $\mathcal{F}$-contraction. Then $\mathcal{T}$ has a unique fixed point $x^* \in \mathcal{X}$ and for every $x_0 \in \mathcal{X}$ a sequence $\mathcal{T}^n x_0 n \in \mathbb{N}$ is convergent to x^*.*

Definition 3.7 ([27]). Let $(\mathcal{X}, d)$ be a metric space and $\mathcal{T} : \mathcal{X} \to CB(\mathcal{X})$ be a mapping. Then $\mathcal{T}$ is a multivalued $\mathcal{F}$-contraction, if $\mathcal{F} \in \Delta(F)$ and there exists $\tau > 0$ such that for all $x, y \in \mathcal{X}$,

$$H(\mathcal{T}x, \mathcal{T}y) > 0 \Rightarrow \tau + \mathcal{F}(H(\mathcal{T}x, \mathcal{T}y)) \leq \mathcal{F}(d(x,y)).$$

Theorem 3.8 ([27]). *Let $(\mathcal{X}, d)$ be a complete metric space and $\mathcal{T} : \mathcal{X} \to K(\mathcal{X})$ be a multivalued $\mathcal{F}$-contraction, then $\mathcal{T}$ has a fixed point in $\mathcal{X}$.*

Theorem 3.9 ([27]). *Let $(\mathcal{X}, d)$ be a complete metric space and $\mathcal{T} : \mathcal{X} \to C(\mathcal{X})$ be a multivalued $\mathcal{F}$-contraction. Suppose $\mathcal{F} \in \Delta(F_*)$, then $\mathcal{T}$ has a fixed point in $\mathcal{X}$.*

For more in this direction, see, [28–31]. Here, we give the concept of multivalued α-F-weak-contractions and prove some fixed point results.

Definition 3.10 Let $\mathcal{T} : \mathcal{X} \to 2^{\mathcal{X}}$ be a multivalued mapping on a metric space $(\mathcal{X}, d)$, then $\mathcal{T}$ is said to be an multivalued α-F-weak-contraction on $\mathcal{X}$, if there exists $\sigma > 0$, $\tau : (0, \infty) \to (\sigma, \infty)$, $\mathcal{F} \in \Delta(F)$ and $\alpha : \mathcal{X} \times \mathcal{X} \to [0, +\infty)$ such that for all $z \in \mathcal{X}, y \in F_\sigma^z$ with $D(z, \mathcal{T}z) > 0$ satisfying

$$\tau(d(z,y)) + \mathcal{F}(\alpha(z,y)D(y, \mathcal{T}y)) \leq \mathcal{F}(M(z,y)), \tag{28}$$

where,

$$\begin{aligned} M(z,y) = \max\Big\{ & d(z,y), D(z, \mathcal{T}z), D(y, \mathcal{T}y), \frac{D(y, \mathcal{T}z) + D(z, \mathcal{T}y)}{2}, \\ & \frac{D(y, \mathcal{T}y)[1 + D(z, \mathcal{T}z)]}{1 + d(z,y)}, \frac{D(y, \mathcal{T}z)[1 + D(z, \mathcal{T}y)]}{1 + d(z,y)} \Big\}. \end{aligned} \tag{29}$$

and

$$\mathcal{F}_\sigma^z = \{y \in \mathcal{T}z : \mathcal{F}(d(z,y)) \leq \mathcal{F}(D(z, \mathcal{T}z)) + \sigma\}.$$

Note that $\mathcal{F}_\sigma^z \neq \emptyset$ in both cases when $\mathcal{F} \in \Delta(F)$ and $\mathcal{F} \in \Delta(F_*)$ [32].

Definition 3.11 Let $\mathcal{T} : \mathcal{X} \to P(\mathcal{X})$ be a multivalued mapping on a metric space $(\mathcal{X}, d)$, then $\mathcal{T}$ is said to be an multivalued α-F-contraction on $\mathcal{X}$, if there exists $\sigma > 0$, $\tau : (0, \infty) \to (\sigma, \infty)$, $\mathcal{F} \in \Delta(F)$ and $\alpha : \mathcal{X} \times \mathcal{X} \to [0, +\infty)$ such that for all $z \in \mathcal{X}, y \in F_\sigma^z$ with $D(z, \mathcal{T}z) > 0$ satisfying

$$\tau(d(z,y)) + \mathcal{F}(\alpha(z,y)D(y, \mathcal{T}y)) \leq \mathcal{F}(d(x,y)), \tag{30}$$

Theorem 3.12 *Let $(\mathcal{X}, d)$ be a complete metric space and $\mathcal{T} : \mathcal{X} \to K(\mathcal{X})$ be an multivalued α-F-weak-contraction satisfying the following assertions:*

1. *$\mathcal{T}$ is multivalued α-orbital admissible mapping;*
2. *the map $z \to D(z, \mathcal{T}z)$ is lower semi-continuous;*
3. *there exists $z_0 \in \mathcal{X}$ and $z_1 \in \mathcal{T}z_0$ such that $\alpha(z_0, z_1) \geq 1$;*
4. *τ satisfies $\lim_{t \to s^+} \inf \tau(t) > \sigma$ for all $s \geq 0$.*

Then $\mathcal{T}$ has a fixed point in $\mathcal{X}$.

Proof. Let $z_0 \in \mathcal{X}$, since $\mathcal{T}z \in K(\mathcal{X})$ for every $z \in \mathcal{X}$, the set F_σ^z is non-empty for any $\sigma > 0$, then there exists $z_1 \in F_\sigma^{z_0}$ and by hypothesis $\alpha(z_0,z_1) \geq 1$. Assume that $z_1 \notin \mathcal{T}z_1$, otherwise z_1 is the fixed point of $\mathcal{T}$. Then, since $\mathcal{T}z_1$ is closed, $D(z_1,\mathcal{T}z_1) > 0$, so, from (28), we have

$$\tau(d(z_0,z_1)) + \mathcal{F}(\alpha(z_0,z_1)D(z_1,\mathcal{T}z_1)) \leq \mathcal{F}(M(z_0,z_1)), \tag{31}$$

where

$$\begin{aligned} M(z_0,z_1) = \max\Bigg\{ & d(z_0,z_1), D(z_0,\mathcal{T}z_0), D(z_1,\mathcal{T}z_1), \frac{D(z_1,\mathcal{T}z_0)+D(z_0,\mathcal{T}z_1)}{2}, \\ & \frac{D(z_1,\mathcal{T}z_1)[1+D(z_0,\mathcal{T}z_0)]}{1+d(z_0,z_1)}, \frac{D(z_1,\mathcal{T}z_0)[1+D(z_0,\mathcal{T}z_1)]}{1+d(z_0,z_1)}\Bigg\}. \end{aligned} \tag{32}$$

Since $\mathcal{T}z_0$ and $\mathcal{T}z_1$ are compact, so we have

$$\begin{aligned} M(z_0,z_1) &= \max\Bigg\{ d(z_0,z_1), d(z_0,z_1), d(z_1,z_2), \frac{d(z_1,z_1)+d(z_0,z_2)}{2}, \\ &\qquad \frac{d(z_1,z_2)[1+d(z_0,z_1)]}{1+d(z_0,z_1)}, \frac{d(z_1,z_1)[1+d(z_0,z_2)]}{1+d(z_0,z_1)}\Bigg\} \\ &= \max\left\{ d(z_0,z_1), d(z_1,z_2), \frac{d(z_0,z_2)}{2}\right\}. \end{aligned} \tag{33}$$

Since $\frac{d(z_0,z_2)}{2} \leq \frac{d(z_0,z_1)+d(z_1,z_2)}{2} \leq \max\{d(z_0,z_1), d(z_1,z_2)\}$, it follows that

$$M(z_0,z_1) \leq \max\{d(z_0,z_1), d(z_1,z_2)\}. \tag{34}$$

Suppose that $d(z_0,z_1) < d(z_1,z_2)$, then (31) implies that

$$\begin{aligned} \tau(d(z_0,z_1)) + \mathcal{F}(D(z_1,\mathcal{T}z_1)) &\leq \tau(d(z_0,z_1)) + \mathcal{F}(\alpha(z_0,z_1)D(z_1,\mathcal{T}z_1)) \\ &\leq \mathcal{F}(d(z_1,z_2)), \end{aligned} \tag{35}$$

consequently,

$$\tau(d(z_0,z_1)) + \mathcal{F}(d(z_1,z_2)) \leq \mathcal{F}(d(z_1,z_2)), \tag{36}$$

or, $\mathcal{F}(d(z_1,z_2)) \leq \mathcal{F}(d(z_1,z_2)) - \tau(d(z_0,z_1))$, which is a contradiction. Hence $M(d(z_0,z_1)) \leq d(z_0,z_1)$, therefore by using (F_1), (31) implies that

$$\tau(d(z_0,z_1)) + \mathcal{F}(\alpha(z_0,z_1)d(z_1,z_2)) \leq \mathcal{F}(d(z_0,z_1)). \tag{37}$$

On continuing recursively, we get a sequence $\{z_n\}_{n\in\mathbb{N}}$ in $\mathcal{X}$, where $z_{n+1} \in F_\sigma^{z_n}$, $z_{n+1} \notin \mathcal{T}z_{n+1}$, $\alpha(z_n,z_{n+1}) \geq 1$, $M(z_n,z_{n+1}) \leq d(z_n,z_{n+1})$ and

$$\tau(d(z_n,z_{n+1})) + \mathcal{F}(D(z_{n+1},\mathcal{T}z_{n+1})) \leq \mathcal{F}(d(z_n,z_{n+1})). \tag{38}$$

Since $z_{n+1} \in F_\sigma^{z_n}$ and $\mathcal{T}z_n$ and $\mathcal{T}z_{n+1}$ are compact, we have

$$\tau(d(z_n,z_{n+1})) + \mathcal{F}(d(z_{n+1},z_{n+2})) \leq \mathcal{F}(d(z_n,z_{n+1})) \tag{39}$$

and

$$\mathcal{F}(d(z_n, z_{n+1})) \leq \mathcal{F}(d(z_n, z_{n+1})) + \sigma. \tag{40}$$

Combining (39) and (40) gives

$$\mathcal{F}(d(z_{n+1}, z_{n+2})) \leq \mathcal{F}(d(z_n, z_{n+1})) + \sigma - \tau(d(z_n, z_{n+1})) \tag{41}$$

Let $d_n = d(z_n, z_{n+1})$ for $n \in \mathbb{N}$, then $d_n > 0$ and from (41) $\{d_n\}$ is decreasing. Therefore, there exists $\delta \geq 0$ such that $\lim_{n\to\infty} d_n = \delta$. Now let $\delta > 0$. From (41), we get

$$\begin{aligned} \mathcal{F}(d_{n+1}) &\leq \mathcal{F}(d_n) + \sigma - \tau(d_n) \leq \mathcal{F}(d_{n-1}) + 2\sigma - \tau(d_n) - \tau(d_{n-1}) \cdots \\ &\leq \mathcal{F}(d_0) + n\sigma - \tau(d_n) - \tau(d_{n-1}) - \cdots - \tau(d_0). \end{aligned} \tag{42}$$

Let $\tau(d_{p_n}) = \min\{\tau(d_0), \tau(d_1), \cdots, \tau(d_n)\}$ for all $n \in \mathbb{N}$. From (42), we get

$$\mathcal{F}(d_{n+1}) \leq \mathcal{F}(d_0) + n(\sigma - \tau(d_{p_n})). \tag{43}$$

From (38), we also get

$$\mathcal{F}(D(z_{n+1}, Tz_{n+1})) \leq \mathcal{F}(D(z_0, Tz_0)) + n(\sigma - \tau(d_{p_n})). \tag{44}$$

Now consider the sequence $\{\tau(d_{p_n})\}$. We distinguish two cases.

Case 1. For each $n \in \mathbb{N}$, there is $m > n$ such that $\tau(d_{p_n}) > \tau(d_{p_m})$. Then we obtain a subsequence $\left\{d_{p_{n_k}}\right\}$ of $\{d_{p_n}\}$ with $\tau\left(d_{p_{n_k}}\right) > \tau\left(d_{p_{n_{k+1}}}\right)$ for all k. Since $d_{p_{n_k}} \to \delta^+$, we deduce that $\lim_{k\to\infty} \inf \tau\left(d_{p_{n_k}}\right) > \sigma$. Hence $\mathcal{F}(d_{n_k}) \leq \mathcal{F}(d_0) + n\left(\sigma - \tau\left(d_{p_{n_k}}\right)\right)$ for all k. Consequently, $\lim_{k\to\infty} \mathcal{F}(d_{n_k}) = -\infty$ and by $(\mathcal{F}_2)$, we obtain $\lim_{k\to\infty} d_{p_{n_k}}) = 0$, which contradicts that $\lim_{n\to\infty} d_n > 0$.

Case 2. There is $n_0 \in \mathbb{N}$ such that $\tau\left(d_{p_{n_0}}\right) > \tau(d_{p_m})$ for all $m > n_0$. Then $\mathcal{F}(d_m) \leq \mathcal{F}(d_0) + m\left(\sigma - \tau\left(d_{p_{n_0}}\right)\right)$ for all $m > n_0$. Hence $\lim_{m\to\infty} \mathcal{F}(d_m) = -\infty$, so $\lim_{m\to\infty} d_m = 0$, which contradicts that $\lim_{m\to\infty} d_m > 0$. Thus,

$$\lim_{n\to\infty} d_n = 0.$$

From $(\mathcal{F}_3)$, there exists $0 < r < 1$ such that $\lim_{n\to\infty} (d_n)^r \mathcal{F}(d_n) = 0$. By (43), we get for all $n \in \mathbb{N}$

$$(d_n)^r \mathcal{F}(d_n) - (d_n)^r \mathcal{F}(d_0) \leq (d_n)^r n(\sigma - \tau(d - p_n)) \leq 0. \tag{45}$$

Letting $n \to \infty$ in (45), we obtain $\lim_{n\to\infty} n(d_n)^r = 0$. This implies that there exists $n_1 \in \mathbb{N}$ such that $n(d_n)^r \leq 1$, or, $d_n \leq \frac{1}{n^{1/r}}$, for all $n > n_1$. Next, for $m > n \geq n_1$ we have

$$d(z_n, z_m) \leq \sum_{i=n}^{m-1} d(z_i, z_{i+1}) \leq \sum_{i=n}^{m-1} \frac{1}{i^{1/k}},$$

since $0 < k < 1$, $\sum_{i=n}^{m-1} \frac{1}{i^{1/k}}$ converges. Therefore, $d(z_n, z_m) \to 0$ as $m, n \to \infty$. Thus, $\{z_n\}$ is a Cauchy sequence. Since $\mathcal{X}$ is complete, there exists $z^* \in \mathcal{X}$ such that $z_n \to z^*$ as $n \to \infty$. From Eqs. (44) and (F_2), we have $\lim_{n\to\infty} D(z_n, Tz_n) = 0$. Since $z \to D(z, Tz)$ is lower semi-continuous, then

$$0 \leq D(z, Tz) \leq \lim_{n\to\infty} \inf D(z_n, Tz_n) = 0.$$

Thus, $\mathcal{T}$ has a fixed point. □

In the following theorem we take $C(\mathcal{X})$ instead of $K(\mathcal{X})$, then we need to take $\mathcal{F}\in\Delta(F_*)$ in Definition 3.10.

Theorem 3.13 *Let $(\mathcal{X},d)$ be a complete metric space and $\mathcal{T}:\mathcal{X}\to C(\mathcal{X})$ be an multivalued α-F-weak-contraction with $\mathcal{F}\in\Delta(F_*)$ satisfying all the assertions of Theorem 3.12. Then $\mathcal{T}$ has a fixed point in $\mathcal{X}$.*

Proof. Let $z_0\in\mathcal{X}$, since $\mathcal{T}z\in C(\mathcal{X})$ for every $z\in\mathcal{X}$ and $\mathcal{F}\in\Delta(F_*)$, the set F_σ^z is non-empty for any $\sigma>0$, then there exists $z_1\in F_\sigma^{z_0}$ and by hypothesis $\alpha(z_0,z_1)\geq 1$. Assume that $z_1\notin\mathcal{T}z_1$, otherwise z_1 is the fixed point of $\mathcal{T}$. Then, since $\mathcal{T}z_1$ is closed, $D(z_1,\mathcal{T}z_1)>0$, so, from (28), we have

$$\tau(d(z_0,z_1))+\alpha(z_0,z_1)\mathcal{F}(D(z_1,\mathcal{T}z_1))\leq\mathcal{F}(M(z_0,z_1)), \tag{46}$$

where

$$\begin{aligned}M(z_0,z_1)=\max\Big\{&d(z_0,z_1),D(z_0,\mathcal{T}z_0),D(z_1,\mathcal{T}z_1),\frac{D(z_1,\mathcal{T}z_0)+D(z_0,\mathcal{T}z_1)}{2},\\&\frac{D(z_1,\mathcal{T}z_1)[1+D(z_0,\mathcal{T}z_0)]}{1+d(z_0,z_1)},\frac{D(z_1,\mathcal{T}z_0)[1+D(z_0,\mathcal{T}z_1)]}{1+d(z_0,z_1)}\Big\}.\end{aligned} \tag{47}$$

The rest of the proof can be completed as in the proof of Theorem 3.12 by considering the closedness of $\mathcal{T}z$, for all $z\in\mathcal{X}$. □

Theorem 3.14 *Let $(\mathcal{X},d)$ be a complete metric space, $\mathcal{T}:\mathcal{X}\to K(\mathcal{X})$ be a continuous mapping and $\mathcal{F}\in\Delta(F)$. Assume that the following assertions hold:*

1. *$\mathcal{T}$ is generalized α_*-admissible mapping;*

2. *there exists $z_0\in\mathcal{X}$ and $z_1\in\mathcal{T}z_0$ such that $\alpha(z_0,z_1)\geq 1$;*

3. *there exists $\tau:(0,\infty)\to(0,\infty)$ such that*

$$\liminf_{t\to s^+}\tau(t)>0 \qquad \text{for all} \quad s\geq 0$$

and for all $z\in\mathcal{X}$ with $H(\mathcal{T}z,\mathcal{T}y)>0$, there exist a function $\alpha:\mathcal{X}\times\mathcal{X}\to\{-\infty\}\cup(0,+\infty)$ satisfying

$$\tau(d(z,y))+\alpha(z,y)\mathcal{F}(H(\mathcal{T}z,\mathcal{T}y))\leq\mathcal{F}(M(z,y)), \tag{48}$$

where $M(z,y)$ is defined in (29).

Then $\mathcal{T}$ has a fixed point in $\mathcal{X}$.

Proof. By following the steps in the proof of Theorem 3.12, we get the required result. □

Note that Theorem 3.14 cannot be obtained from Theorem 3.12, because in Theorem 3.12, σ cannot be equal to zero.

Theorem 3.15 *Let $(\mathcal{X},d)$ be a complete metric space, $\mathcal{T}:\mathcal{X}\to C(\mathcal{X})$ be a continuous mapping and $\mathcal{F}\in\Delta(F_*)$ satisfying all assertions of Theorem 3.14. Then $\mathcal{T}$ has a fixed point in $\mathcal{X}$.*

From Theorems 3.14 and 3.15, we get the following fixed point result for single valued mappings:

Theorem 3.16 *Let $(\mathcal{X},d)$ be a complete metric space, $\mathcal{T}:\mathcal{X}\to\mathcal{X}$ be a continuous mapping and $\mathcal{F}\in\Delta(F)$. Assume that the following assertions hold:*

1. *$\mathcal{T}$ is α-admissible mapping;*

2. *there exists* $z_0, z_1 \in \mathcal{X}$ *such that* $\alpha(z_0, z_1) \geq 1$;

3. *there exists* $\tau : (0,\infty) \to (0,\infty)$ *such that*

$$\liminf_{t \to s^+} \tau(t) > 0 \qquad \text{for all} \quad s \geq 0$$

and for all $z \in \mathcal{X}$ with $d(\mathcal{T}z, \mathcal{T}y) > 0$, there exist a function $\alpha : \mathcal{X} \times \mathcal{X} \to \{-\infty\} \cup (0, +\infty)$ satisfying

$$\tau(d(z,y)) + \alpha(z,y)\mathcal{F}(d(\mathcal{T}z, \mathcal{T}y)) \leq \mathcal{F}(m(z,y)), \tag{49}$$

where

$$m(z,y) = \max\left\{d(z,y), d(z,\mathcal{T}z), d(y,\mathcal{T}y), \frac{d(y,\mathcal{T}z)+d(z,\mathcal{T}y)}{2}, \frac{d(y,\mathcal{T}y)[1+d(z,\mathcal{T}z)]}{1+d(z,y)}, \frac{d(y,\mathcal{T}z)[1+d(z,\mathcal{T}y)]}{1+d(z,y)}\right\}. \tag{50}$$

Then $\mathcal{T}$ *has a fixed point in* $\mathcal{X}$.

Now, let $(\mathcal{X}, d, \preccurlyeq)$ be a partially ordered metric space. Recall that $\mathcal{T} : \mathcal{X} \to 2^{\mathcal{X}}$ is monotone increasing if $\mathcal{T}y \preccurlyeq \mathcal{T}z$ for all $y, z \in \mathcal{X}$, for which $y \preccurlyeq z$ (see [33]). There are many applications in differential and integral equations of monotone mappings in ordered metric spaces (see [34–36] and references therein).

Theorem 3.17 *Let* $(\mathcal{X}, d, \preccurlyeq)$ *be a complete partially ordered metric space and let* $\mathcal{T} : \mathcal{X} \to 2^{\mathcal{X}}$ *be a closed valued mapping satisfying the following assertions for all* $y, z \in \mathcal{X}$ *with* $y \preccurlyeq z$:

1. $\mathcal{T}$ *is monotone increasing;*

2. $\vartheta(H(\mathcal{T}y, \mathcal{T}z), d(y,z)) \geq 0$;

3. *there exists* $z_0 \in X$ *and* $z_1 \in \mathcal{T}z_0$ *such that* $z_0 \preccurlyeq z_1$;

4. *for a sequence* $\{z_n\} \subset \mathcal{X}$, $\lim_{n\to\infty}\{z_n\} = z$ *and* $z_n \preccurlyeq z_{n+1}$ *for all* $n \in \mathbb{N}$, *we have* $z_n \preccurlyeq z$ *for all* $n \in \mathbb{N}$.

Then $Fix\{\mathcal{T}\} \neq \varnothing$.

Proof. Define $\alpha, \eta : \mathcal{X} \times \mathcal{X} \to [0, \infty)$ by

$$\alpha(y,z) = \begin{cases} 1 & y \preccurlyeq z \\ 0 & \text{otherwise} \end{cases} \qquad \eta(y,z) = \begin{cases} \frac{1}{2} & y \preccurlyeq z \\ 0 & \text{otherwise,} \end{cases}$$

then for $y, z \in \mathcal{X}$ with $y \preccurlyeq z$, $\alpha(y,z) \geq \eta(y,z)$ implies $\alpha_*(\mathcal{T}y, \mathcal{T}z) = 1 > \frac{1}{2} = \eta_*(\mathcal{T}y, \mathcal{T}z)$ and $\alpha_*(\mathcal{T}y, \mathcal{T}z) = \eta_*(\mathcal{T}y, \mathcal{T}z) = 0$ otherwise. Thus, all the conditions of Theorem 3.4 are satisfied and hence $\mathcal{T}$ has a fixed point. □

In case of single valued mapping Theorem 3.17 reduced to the following:

Theorem 3.18 *Let* $(\mathcal{X}, d, \preccurlyeq)$ *be a complete partially ordered metric space and let* $\mathcal{T} : \mathcal{X} \to \mathcal{X}$ *be a self-map fulfilling the following assertions:*

1. $\mathcal{T}$ *is monotone increasing;*

2. $\vartheta(d(Ty,Tz),d(y,z)) \geq 0$;

3. *there exists* $z_0 \in \mathcal{X}$ *and* $z_1 = Tz_0$ *such that* $z_0 \preccurlyeq z_1$;

4. *for a sequence* $\{z_n\} \subset \mathcal{X}$, $\lim_{n\to\infty}\{z_n\} = z$ *and* $z_n \preccurlyeq z_{n+1}$ *for all* $n \in \mathbb{N}$, *we have* $z_n \preccurlyeq z$ *for all* $n \in \mathbb{N}$.

for all $y, z \in \mathcal{X}$ with $y \preccurlyeq z$ and $\vartheta \in \widehat{Man(\mathbb{R})}$. Then $Fix\{T\} \neq \emptyset$.

Definition 3.19 Let $T : \mathcal{X} \to 2^{\mathcal{X}}$ be a multivalued mapping on a partially ordered metric space $(\mathcal{X}, d, \preccurlyeq)$, then T is said to be an ordered $\mathcal{F}$-τ-contraction on $\mathcal{X}$, if there exists $\sigma > 0$ and $\tau : (0,\infty) \to (\sigma,\infty)$, $\mathcal{F} \in \Delta(F)$ such that for all $z \in \mathcal{X}$, $y \in \mathcal{F}_\sigma^z$ with $z \preccurlyeq y$ and $D(z,Tz) > 0$ satisfying

$$\tau(d(z,y)) + \mathcal{F}(D(y,Ty)) \leq \mathcal{F}(M(z,y)), \tag{51}$$

where,

$$M(z,y) = \max\left\{ d(z,y), D(z,Tz), D(y,Ty), \frac{D(y,Tz)+D(z,Ty)}{2}, \frac{D(y,Ty)[1+D(z,Tz)]}{1+d(z,y)}, \frac{D(y,Tz)[1+D(z,Ty)]}{1+d(z,y)} \right\}. \tag{52}$$

Theorem 3.20 *Let* $(\mathcal{X}, d, \preccurlyeq)$ *be a complete partially ordered metric space and* $T : \mathcal{X} \to K(\mathcal{X})$ *be an ordered* $\mathcal{F}$-τ-*contraction satisfying the following assertions:*

1. T *is monotone increasing;*

2. *the map* $z \to D(z,Tz)$ *is lower semi-continuous;*

3. *there exists* $z_0 \in \mathcal{X}$ *and* $z_1 \in Tz_0$ *such that* $z_0 \preccurlyeq z_1$;

4. τ *satisfies*

$$\liminf_{t\to s^+} \tau(t) > \sigma \qquad \text{for all} \quad s \geq 0$$

Then T *has a fixed point in* $\mathcal{X}$.

Proof. By using the similar arguments as in the proof of Theorem 3.17 and using Theorem 3.12, we get the result. □

Theorem 3.21 *Let* $(\mathcal{X}, d, \preccurlyeq)$ *be a complete partially ordered metric space and* $T : \mathcal{X} \to C(\mathcal{X})$ *be an ordered* $\mathcal{F}$-τ-*contraction with* $\mathcal{F} \in \Delta(F_*)$ *satisfying all the assertions of Theorem 3.20. Then* T *has a fixed point in* $\mathcal{X}$.

Theorem 3.22 *Let* $(\mathcal{X}, d, \preccurlyeq)$ *be a complete partially ordered metric space,* $T : \mathcal{X} \to K(\mathcal{X})$ *be a continuous mapping and* $\mathcal{F} \in \Delta(F)$. *Assume that the following assertions hold:*

1. T *is monotone increasing;*

2. *there exists* $z_0 \in \mathcal{X}$ *and* $z_1 \in Tz_0$ *such that* $z_0 \preccurlyeq z_1$;

3. *there exists* $\tau : (0,\infty) \to (0,\infty)$ *such that*

$$\liminf_{t\to s^+} \tau(t) > 0 \qquad \text{for all} \quad s \geq 0$$

and for all $z, y \in \mathcal{X}$ with $z \preccurlyeq y$ and $H(\mathcal{T}z, \mathcal{T}y) > 0$ satisfying

$$\tau(d(z,y)) + \mathcal{F}(H(\mathcal{T}z, \mathcal{T}y)) \leq \mathcal{F}(M(z,y)), \tag{53}$$

where $M(z,y)$ is defined in (52).

Then $\mathcal{T}$ has a fixed point in $\mathcal{X}$.

Proof. By defining $\alpha : \mathcal{X} \times \mathcal{X} \to [0, \infty)$ as in the proof of Theorem 3.17 and by using Theorem (3.14), we get the required result. □

Theorem 3.23 *Let $(\mathcal{X}, d, \preccurlyeq)$ be a complete partially ordered metric space, $\mathcal{T} : \mathcal{X} \to C(\mathcal{X})$ be a continuous mapping and $\mathcal{F} \in \Delta(F_*)$ satisfying all assertions of Theorem 3.22. Then $\mathcal{T}$ has a fixed point in $\mathcal{X}$.*

From Theorems 3.22 and 3.23, we get the following fixed point result for single valued mapping.

Theorem 3.24 *Let $(\mathcal{X}, d, \preccurlyeq)$ be a complete partially ordered metric space, $\mathcal{T} : \mathcal{X} \to \mathcal{X}$ be a continuous mapping and $\mathcal{F} \in \Delta(F)$. Assume that the following assertions hold:*

1. *$\mathcal{T}$ is monotone increasing;*

2. *there exists $z_0, z_1 \in \mathcal{X}$ such that $z_0 \preccurlyeq z_1$;*

3. *there exists $\tau : (0, \infty) \to (0, \infty)$ such that*

$$\liminf_{t \to s^+} \tau(t) > 0 \qquad \text{for all} \quad s \geq 0$$

and for all $z, y \in \mathcal{X}$ with $z \preccurlyeq y$ and $d(\mathcal{T}z, \mathcal{T}y) > 0$ satisfying

$$\tau(d(z,y)) + \mathcal{F}(d(\mathcal{T}z, \mathcal{T}y)) \leq \mathcal{F}(m(z,y)), \tag{54}$$

where

$$\begin{aligned} m(z,y) = \max\Bigg\{ & d(z,y), d(z, \mathcal{T}z), d(y, \mathcal{T}y), \frac{d(y, \mathcal{T}z) + d(z, \mathcal{T}y)}{2}, \\ & \frac{d(y, \mathcal{T}y)[1 + d(z, \mathcal{T}z)]}{1 + d(z,y)}, \frac{d(y, \mathcal{T}z)[1 + d(z, \mathcal{T}y)]}{1 + d(z,y)} \Bigg\}. \end{aligned} \tag{55}$$

Then $\mathcal{T}$ has a fixed point in $\mathcal{X}$.

4. Existence of solution

In this section, by using the fixed point results proved in the previous section, we obtain the existence of the solution of integral Eq. (2) and matrix Eq. (1).

4.1 Solution of Fredholm integral equation of second kind

Let $\ll$ be a partial order relation on $\mathbb{R}^n$. Define $\mathcal{T} : \mathcal{X} \to \mathcal{X}$ by

$$\mathcal{T}z(r) = \int_b^c \mathcal{B}(r, s, z(s)) ds + g(r), \qquad r \in [a, b]. \tag{56}$$

Theorem 4.1 *Let $\mathcal{X} = C([b, c], \mathbb{R}^n)$ with the usual spermium norm. Suppose that*
1. $\mathcal{B} : [b, c] \times [b, c] \times \mathbb{R}^n \to \mathbb{R}^n$ and $g : \mathbb{R}^n \to \mathbb{R}^n$ are continuous;

2. there exists a continuous function $p : [b,c] \times [b,c] \to [b,c]$ such that

$$|\mathcal{B}(r,s,u) - \mathcal{B}(r,s,v)| \le p(r,s)|u - v|, \tag{57}$$

for each $r, s \in [b,c]$ and $u, v \in \mathbb{R}^n$ with $u \ll v$.
3. $\sup_{r\in[b,c]} \int_b^c p(r,s)ds = q \le \frac{1}{4}$;
4. there exists $z_0 \in \mathcal{X}$ and $z_1 \in \mathcal{T}z_0$ such that $z_0 \preccurlyeq z_1$;
5. for a sequence $\{z_n\} \subset \mathcal{X}$, $\lim_{n\to\infty}\{z_n\} = z$ and $z_n \preccurlyeq z_{n+1}$ for all $n \in \mathbb{N}$, we have $z_n \preccurlyeq z$ for all $n \in \mathbb{N}$.

Then the integral Eq. (2) has a solution in $\mathcal{X}$.

Proof. Let $\mathcal{X} = C([b,c], \mathbb{R}^n)$ and $\|z\| = \max_{r\in[b,c]}|z(r)|$, for $z \in C([a,b])$. Consider a partial order defined on $\mathcal{X}$ by

$$y, z \in C([b,c], \mathbb{R}^n), \quad y \preccurlyeq z \quad \text{if and only if} \quad y(r) \ll z(r), \ \textit{for} \ r \in [b,c]. \tag{58}$$

Then $(\mathcal{X}, \|.\|, \preccurlyeq)$ is a complete partial ordered metric space and for any increasing sequence $\{z_n\}$ in $\mathcal{X}$ converging to $z \in \mathcal{X}$, we have $z_n(r) \ll z(r)$ for any $r \in [b,c]$ (see [36]). By using Eq. (56), conditions (2, 3) and taking $\vartheta(r,s) = \frac{1}{2}s - r$ for all $y, z \in \mathcal{X}$ with $y \preccurlyeq z$, we obtain

$$\begin{aligned}
|\mathcal{T}y(r) - \mathcal{T}z(r)| &= \left|\int_b^c \mathcal{B}(r,s,y(s))ds - \int_b^c \mathcal{B}(r,s,z(s))ds\right| \\
&\le \int_b^c |\mathcal{B}(r,s,y(s)) - \mathcal{B}(r,s,z(s))|ds \\
&\le \int_b^c p(r,s)|y(s) - z(s)|ds \\
&\le \frac{1}{4}\|y - z\|.
\end{aligned}$$

This implies that

$$\frac{1}{2}\|y - z\| - \|\mathcal{T}y - \mathcal{T}z\| \quad \ge \frac{1}{2}\|y - z\| - \frac{1}{4}\|y - z\| = \frac{1}{4}\|y - z\|.$$

So $\vartheta(d(\mathcal{T}y, \mathcal{T}z), d(y,z)) \ge 0$ for all $y, z \in \mathcal{X}$ with $y \preccurlyeq z$. Hence all the conditions of Theorem 3.18 are satisfied. Therefore $\mathcal{T}$ has a fixed point, consequently, integral Eq. (2) has a solution in $\mathcal{X}$. □

4.2 Solution of non-linear matrix equation

Theorem 4.2 *Let $\gamma : H(n) \to H(n)$ be an order-preserving mapping which maps $P(n)$ into $P(n)$ and $Q \in P(n)$. Assume that there exists a positive number N for which $\sum_{i=1}^m A_i A_i^* \prec N I_n$ and $\sum_{i=1}^m A_i^* \gamma(Q) A_i \succ 0$ such that for all $X \preccurlyeq Y$ we have*

$$d(\gamma(X), \gamma(Y)) \le \frac{1}{N} m(Y,X) e^{-\left(\frac{2+d(X,Y)}{2d(X,Y)}\right)}, \tag{59}$$

where

$$\begin{aligned}
m(X,Y) = \max\Bigg\{ & d(X,Y), d(X,TX), d(Y,TY), \frac{d(Y,TY) + d(X,TX)}{2}, \\
& \frac{d(Y,TY)[1 + d(X,TX)]}{1 + d(X,Y)}, \frac{d(Y,TX)[1 + d(X,TY)]}{1 + d(X,Y)} \Bigg\}.
\end{aligned}$$

Then (1) has a solution in $P(n)$.

Proof. Define $\mathcal{T} : H(n) \to H(n)$ and $\mathcal{F} : \mathbb{R}+ \to \mathbb{R}$ by

$$\mathcal{T}(X) = Q + \sum_{i=1}^{m} A_i^* \gamma(X) A_i \tag{60}$$

and $F(r) = \ln r$ respectively. Then a fixed point of $\mathcal{T}$ is a solution of (1). Let $X, Y \in H(n)$ with $X \preccurlyeq Y$, then $\gamma(X) \preccurlyeq \gamma(y)$. So, for $d(X, Y) > 0$ and $\tau(t) = \frac{1}{t} + \frac{1}{2}$, we have

$$\begin{aligned}
d(TX, TY) &= \|\mathcal{T}Y - \mathcal{T}X\|_1 \\
&= tr(\mathcal{T}Y - \mathcal{T}X) \\
&= \sum_{i=1}^{m} tr(A_i A_i^*(\gamma(Y) - \gamma(X))) \\
&= tr\left(\left(\sum_{i=1}^{m} A_i A_i^*\right)(\gamma(Y) - \gamma(X))\right) \\
&\le \left\|\sum_{i=1}^{m} A_i A_i^*\right\| \|\gamma(Y) - \gamma(X)\|_1 \\
&\le \frac{\left\|\sum_{i=1}^{m} A_i A_i^*\right\|}{N} m(Y,X) e^{-\left(\frac{2+\|Y-X\|_1}{2\|Y-X\|_1}\right)} \\
&< m(Y,X) e^{-\left(\frac{2+\|Y-X\|_1}{2\|Y-X\|_1}\right)},
\end{aligned}$$

and so,

$$\ln\left(\|\mathcal{T}Y - \mathcal{T}X\|_1\right) < \ln\left(m(Y,X) e^{-\left(\frac{2+\|Y-X\|_1}{2\|Y-X\|_1}\right)}\right) = \ln\left(m(X,Y)\right) - \frac{2 + \|Y - X\|_1}{2\|Y - X\|_1}.$$

This implies that

$$\frac{1}{\|Y - X\|_1} + \frac{1}{2} + \ln\left(\|\mathcal{T}Y - \mathcal{T}X\|_1\right) < \ln\left(m(X, Y)\right).$$

Consequently,

$$\tau(d(X, Y)) + \mathcal{F}(d(TX, TY)) < \mathcal{F}(m(X, Y)).$$

Also, from $\sum_{i=1}^{m} A_i^* \gamma(Q) A_i \succ 0$, we have $Q \preccurlyeq \mathcal{T}(Q)$. Thus, by using Theorem 3.24, we conclude that $\mathcal{T}$ has a fixed point and hence (1) has a solution in $P(n)$. □

Author details

Nawab Hussain[1]* and Iram Iqbal[2]

1 Department of Mathematics, King Abdulaziz University, Jeddah, Saudi Arabia

2 Department of Mathematics, University of Sargodha, Sargodha, Pakistan

*Address all correspondence to: nhusain@kau.edu.sa

References

[1] Ran ACM, Reurings MCB. A fixed point theorem in partially ordered sets and some applications to matrix equations. Proc Amer Soc. 2004;**132**: 1435-1443

[2] Lim Y. Solving the nonlinear matrix equation $X = \Sigma_{i=1}^{m} M_i X^{\delta_i} M_i^*$ via a contraction principle. Linear Algebra and its Applications. 2009;**430**: 1380-1383

[3] Berzig M, Samet B. Solving systems of nonlinear matrix equations involving Lipshitzian mappings. Fixed Point Theory and Applications. 2011;**2011**: 1-10

[4] Hussain N, Ahmad J, Ciric L, Azam A. Coincidence point theorems for generalized contractions with application to integral equations. Fixed Point Theory and Applications. 2015:78

[5] Hussain N, Taoudi MA. Krasnosel'skii-type fixed point theorems with applications to Volterra integral equations. Fixed Point Theory and Applications. 2013:196

[6] Hussain N, Azam A, Ahmad J, Arshad M. Common fixed point results in complex valued metric spaces with application to integral equations. Filomat. 2014;**28**(7):1363-1380

[7] Hussain N, Parvaneh V, Roshan JR. Fixed point results for G-α-contractive maps with application to boundary value problems. The Scientific World Journal. 2014. Article ID 585964

[8] Hussain N, Salimi P, Vetro P. Fixed points for Suzuki-φ-ψ-contractions with applications to integral equations. Carpathian Journal of Mathematics. 2014;**30**(2):197-207

[9] Hussain N, Kutbi MA, Roshan JR, Parvaneh V. Coupled and tripled coincidence point results with application to Fredholm integral equations. Abstract and Applied Analysis. 2014:18. Article ID 568718

[10] Hussain N, Salimi P. Fixed points for generalized ψ-contractions with application to integral equations. Journal of Nonlinear and Convex Analysis. 2015:4

[11] Hussain N, Khan AR, Agarwal RP. Krasnosel'skii and Ky Fan type fixed point theorems in ordered Banach spaces. Journal of Nonlinear and Convex Analysis. 2010;**11, 3**:475-489

[12] Khan AR, Kumar V, Hussain N. Analytical and numerical treatment of Jungck-type iterative schemes. Applied Mathematics and Computation. 2014; **231**:521-535

[13] Hussain N, Al-Mezel S, Salimi P. Fixed points for ψ-graphic contractions with application to integral equations. Abstract and Applied Analysis. 2013:11. Article ID 575869

[14] Nieto JJ, Rodríguez-López R, Franco D. Linear first-order fuzzy differential equation. International Journal of Uncertainty, Fuzziness and Knowledge-Based Systems. 2006;**14**:687-709

[15] Ren Y, Zhang B, Qiao H. A simple Taylor-series expansion method for a class of second kind integral equations. Journal of Computational and Applied Mathematics. 1999;**110**:15-24

[16] He JH. Homotopy perturbation technique. Computer Methods in Applied Mechanics and Engineering. 1999:257-262

[17] Wazwaz A. A reliable modification of Adomian decomposition method. Applied Mathematics and Computation. 1999;**102**:77-86

[18] Long G, Nelakanti G. Iteration methods for Fredholm integral equations of the second kind. Computers & Mathematics with Applications. 2007;**53**:886-894

[19] Avazzadeh Z, Heydari M, Loghmani GB. Numerical sulution of Fredholm integral equations of the second kind by using integral mean value theorem. Applied Mathematical Modelling. 2011; **35**:2374-2383

[20] Banach S. Sur les opérations dans les ensembles abstraits et leur application aux équations intégerales. Fundamenta Mathematicae. 1922;**1922**(3):133-181

[21] Nadler SB. Multivalued contraction mappings. Pacific Journal of Mathematics. 1969;**30**:475-488

[22] Hussain N, Salimi P, Latif A. Fixed point results for single and set-valued α-η-ψ-contractive mappings. Fixed Point Theory and Applications. 2013;**2013**. Article ID 212

[23] Ali UM, Kamram T, Sintunavarat W, Katchang P. Mizoguchi-Takahashi's fixed point theorem with α, η functions. Abstract and Applied Analysis. 2013; **2013**. Article ID 418798

[24] Du WS, Khojasteh F. New results and generalizations for approximate fixed point property and their applications. Abstract and Applied Analysis. 2014;**2014**. Article ID 581267

[25] Hussain N, Ahmad J, Azam A. On Suzuki-Wardowski type fixed point theorems. Journal of Nonlinear Sciences and Applications. 2015;**8**:1095-1111

[26] Wardowski D. Fixed points of a new type of contractive mappings in complete metric spaces. Fixed Point Theory and Applications. 2012:94

[27] Altun I, Minak G, Dağ H. Multivalued F-contractions on complete metric space. Journal of Nonlinear and Convex Analysis. 2015;**16**:659-666

[28] Hussain N, Latif A, Iqbal I. Fixed point results for generalized, F-contractions in modular metric and fuzzy metric spaces. Fixed Point Theory and Applications. 2015:158

[29] Wardowski D, Dung NV. Fixed points of F-weak contractions on complete metric space. Demonstratio Mathematica. 2014;**47**:146-155

[30] Iqbal I, Hussain N. Fixed point theorems for generalized multivalued nonlinear $\mathcal{F}$-contractions. Journal of Nonlinear Sciences and Applications. 2016;**9**:5870-5893

[31] Hussain N, Iqbal I. Global best approximate solutions for set-valued cyclic α-F-contractions. Journal of Nonlinear Sciences and Applications. 2017;**10**:5090-5107

[32] Minak G, Olgun M, Altun I. A new approach to fixed point theorems for multivalued contractive maps. Carpathian Journal of Mathematics. 2015;**31, 2**:241-248

[33] Dhage BC. Hybrid fixed point theory for right monotone increasing multi-valued mappings and neutral functional differential inclusions. Archivum Mathematicum (BRNO) Tomus. 2007;**43**:265-284

[34] Agarwal RP, Hussain N, Taoudi MA. Fixed point theorems in ordered Banach spaces and applications to nonlinear integral equations. Abstract and Applied Analysis. 2012;**2012**:15. Article ID 245872

[35] Ansari QH, Idzik A, Yao JC. Coincidence and fixed point theorems with applications. Topological Methods in Nonlinear Analysis. 2000;**15**(1): 191-202

[36] Hussain N, Kutbi MA, Salimi P. Fixed point theory in α-complete metric spaces with applications. Abstract and Applied Analysis. 2014:11. Article ID 280817

Section 3

Advanced Themes of Integral Equations

Chapter 3

A Probabilistic Interpretation of Nonlinear Integral Equations

Isamu Dôku

Abstract

We study a probabilistic interpretation of solutions to a class of nonlinear integral equations. By considering a branching model and defining a star-product, we construct a tree-based star-product functional as a probabilistic solution of the integral equation. Although the original integral equation has nothing to do with a stochastic world, some probabilistic technique enables us not only to relate the deterministic world with the stochastic one but also to interpret the equation as a random quantity. By studying mathematical structure of the constructed functional, we prove that the function given by expectation of the functional with respect to the law of a branching process satisfies the original integral equation.

Keywords: nonlinear integral equation, branching model, tree structure, star-product, probabilistic solution

AMS classification: Primary 45G10; Secondary 60 J80, 60 J85, 60 J57

1. Introduction

This chapter treats a topic on probabilistic representations of solutions to a certain class of deterministic nonlinear integral equations. Indeed, this is a short review article to introduce the star-product functional and a probabilistic construction of solutions to nonlinear integral equations treated in [1]. The principal parts for the existence and uniqueness of solutions are taken from [1] with slight modification. Since the nonlinear integral equations which we handle are deterministic, they have nothing to do with random world. Hence, we assume that an integral formula may hold, which plays an essential role in connecting a deterministic world with a random one. Once this relationship has been established, we begin with constructing a branching model and we are able to construct a star-product functional based upon the model. At the end we prove that the function provided by the expectation of the functional with respect to the law of a branching process in question solves the original integral equations (see also [2–4]).

More precisely, in this chapter we consider the deterministic nonlinear integral equation of the type:

$$
\begin{aligned}
e^{\lambda t|x|^2}u(t,x) &= u_0(x) + \frac{\lambda}{2}\int_0^t ds\, e^{\lambda s|x|^2}\int p(s,x,y;u)n(x,y)\,dy \\
&\quad + \frac{\lambda}{2}\int_0^t e^{\lambda s|x|^2} f(s,x)\,ds.
\end{aligned} \tag{1}
$$

One of the reasons why we are interested in this kind of integral equations consists in its importance in applicatory fields, especially in mathematical physics. For instance, in quantum physics or applied mathematics, a variety of differential equations have been dealt with by many researchers (e.g., [5, 6]), and in most cases, their integral forms have been discussed more than their differential forms on a practical basis. There can be found plenty of integral equations similar to Eq. (1) appearing in mathematical physics.

The purpose of this article is to provide with a quite general method of giving a probabilistic interpretation to deterministic equations. Any deterministic representation of the solutions to Eq. (1) has not been known yet in analysis. The main contents of the study consist in derivation of the probabilistic representation of the solutions to Eq. (1). Our mathematical model is a kind of generalization of the integral equations that were treated in [7], and our kernel appearing in Eq. (1) is given in a more abstract setting. We are aiming at establishment of new probabilistic representations of the solutions.

This paper is organized as follows: In Section 2 we introduce notations which are used in what follows. In Section 3 principal results are stated, where we refer the probabilistic representation of the solutions to a class of deterministic nonlinear integral equations in question. Section 4 deals with branching model and its treelike structure. Section 5 treats construction of star-product functional based upon those tree structures of branching model described in the previous section. The proof of the main theorem will be stated in Sections 6 and 7. Section 6 provides with the proof of existence of the probabilistic solutions to the integral equations. We also consider *-product functional, which is a sister functional of the star-product functional. This newly presented functionals play an essential role in governing the behaviors of star-product functionals via control inequality. Section 7 deals with the proof of uniqueness for the constructed solutions, in terms of the martingale theory [8].

We think that it would not be enough to derive simply explicit representations of probabilistic solutions to the equations, but it is extremely important to make use of the formulae practically in the problem of computations. We hope that our result shall be a trigger to further development on the study in this direction.

2. Notations

Let $D_0 := \mathbb{R}^3 \ \{0\}$ and $\mathbb{R}_+ := [0, \infty)$. For every $\alpha, \beta \in \mathbb{C}^3$, the symbol $\alpha \cdot \beta$ means the inner product, and we define $e_x := x/|x|$ for every $x \in D_0$. We consider the following deterministic nonlinear integral equation:

$$\begin{aligned} e^{\lambda t|x|^2} u(t,x) &= u_0(x) + \frac{\lambda}{2}\int_0^t \mathrm{d}s\, e^{\lambda s|x|^2} \int p(s,x,y;u) n(x,y) \mathrm{d}y \\ &\quad + \frac{\lambda}{2}\int_0^t e^{\lambda s|x|^2} f(s,x) s, \quad \text{for} \quad \forall (t,x) \in \mathbb{R}_+ \times D_0. \end{aligned} \tag{2}$$

Here, $u \equiv u(t,x)$ is an unknown function: $\mathbb{R}_+ \times D_0 \to \mathbb{C}^3$, $\lambda > 0$, and $u_0 : D_0 \to \mathbb{C}^3$ are the initial data such that $u(t,x)|_{t=0} = u_0(x)$. Moreover, $f(t,x)$: $\mathbb{R}_+ \times D_0 \to \mathbb{C}^3$ is a given function satisfying $f(t,x)/|x|^2 =: \tilde{f} \in L^1(\mathbb{R}_+)$ for each $x \in D_0$. The integrand p in Eq. (2) is actually given by

$$p(t,x,y;u) = u(t,y) \cdot e_x \{u(t,x-y) - e_x (u(t,x-y) \cdot e_x)\}. \tag{3}$$

Suppose that the integral kernel $n(x,y)$ is bounded and measurable with respect to $x \times y$. On the other hand, we consider a Markov kernel $K\colon D_0 \to D_0 \times D_0$. Namely, for every $z \in D_0$, $K_z(x,y)$ lies in the space $\mathcal{P}(D_0 \times D_0)$ of all probability measures on a product space $D_0 \times D_0$. When the kernel k is given by $k(x,y) = i|x|^{-2} n(x,y)$, then we define K_z as a Markov kernel satisfying that for any positive measurable function $h = h(x,y)$ on $D_0 \times D_0$,

$$\iint h(x,y) K_z(x,y) = \int h(x, z-x) k(x,z) \mathrm{d}x. \tag{4}$$

Moreover, we assume that for every measurable functions $f, g > 0$ on $\mathbb{R}^+$,

$$\int h(|z|)\nu(z) \int g(|x|) K_z(x,y) = \int g(|z|)\nu(z) \int h(|y|) K_z(\mathrm{d}x, \mathrm{d}y) \tag{5}$$

holds, where the measure ν is given by $\nu(dz) = |z|^{-3} dz$.

The equality (Eq. (4)) is not only a simple integral transform formula. In fact, in the analytical point of view, it merely says that the double integral with respect to K_z is changed into a single integral with respect to x just after the execution of iterative integration of $h(x,y)$ with respect to the second parameter y. However, our point here consists in establishing a great bridge between a deterministic world and a stochastic world. The validity of the assumed equality (Eq. (5)) means that a sort of symmetry in a wide sense may be posed on our kernel K.

3. Main results

In this section we shall introduce our main results, which assert the existence and uniqueness of solutions to the nonlinear integral equation. That is to say, we derive a probabilistic representation of the solutions to Eq. (2) by employing the star-product functional. As a matter of fact, the solution $u(t,x)$ can be expressed as the expectation of a star-product functional, which is nothing but a probabilistic solution constructed by making use of the below-mentioned branching particle systems and branching models. Let

$$M_\star^{\langle u_0, f\rangle}(\omega) = \prod \star_{[x\tilde{m}]} \Xi^{m_1}_{m_2.m_3}[u_0, f](\omega), \tag{6}$$

be a probabilistic representation in terms of tree-based star-product functional with weight (u_0, f) (see Section 5 for the details of the definition). On the other hand, $M_*^{\langle U,F\rangle}(\omega)$ denotes the associated *-product functional with weight (U,F), which is indexed by the nodes (x_m) of a binary tree. Here, we suppose that $U = U(x)$ (resp. $F = F(t,x)$) is a nonnegative measurable function on D_0 (resp. $\mathbb{R}_+ \times D_0$), respectively, and also that $F(\cdot, x) \in L^1(\mathbb{R}_+)$ for each x. Indeed, in construction of the *-product functional, the product in question is taken as ordinary multiplication * instead of the star-product $\bigstar$ in the definition of star-product functional.

Theorem 1. *Suppose that* $|u_0(x)| \leqslant U(x)$ *for every* x *and* $|\tilde{f}(t,x)| \leqslant F(t,x)$ *for every* t, x *and also that for some* $T > 0$ ($T > > 1$, *sufficiently large*)

$$E_{T,x}\left[M_*^{\langle U,F\rangle}(\omega)\right] < \infty, \quad \text{a.e.} - x \tag{7}$$

holds. Then, there exists a (u_0,f)*-weighted tree-based star* $\bigstar$*-product functional* $M_{\bigstar}^{\langle u_0 f\rangle}(\omega)$*, indexed by a set of node labels accordingly to the tree structure which a binary critical branching process* $Z^{K_x}(t)$ *determines. Furthermore, the function*

$$u(t,x) = E_{t,x}\left[M_{\bigstar}^{\langle u_0 f\rangle}(\omega)\right] \tag{8}$$

gives a unique solution to the integral equation (Eq. (2)). *Here,* $E_{t,x}$ *denotes the expectation with respect to a probability measure* $P_{t,x}$ *as the time-reversed law of* $Z^{K_x}(t)$.

4. Branching model and its associated treelike structure

In this section we consider a continuous time binary critical branching process $Z^{K_x}(t)$ on D_0 [9], whose branching rate is given by a parameter $\lambda|x|^2$, whose branching mechanism is binary with equiprobability, and whose descendant branching particle behavior is determined by the kernel K_x (cf. [10]). Next, taking notice of the tree structure which the process $Z^{K_x}(t)$ determines, we denote the space of marked trees

$$\omega = (t, (t_m), (x_m), (\eta_m), m \in \mathcal{V}) \tag{9}$$

by Ω (see [11]). We also consider the time-reversed law of $Z^{K_x}(t)$ being a probability measure on Ω as $P_{t,x} \in \mathcal{P}(\Omega)$. Here, t denotes the birth time of common ancestor, and the particle x_m dies when $\eta_m = 0$, while it generates two descendants x_{m1}, x_{m2} when $\eta_m = 1$. On the other hand,

$$\mathcal{V} = \bigcup_{\ell \geq 0} \{1, 2\}^{\ell}$$

is a set of all labels, namely, finite sequences of symbols with length ℓ, which describe the whole tree structure given [12]. For $\omega \in \Omega$ we denote by $\mathcal{N}(\omega)$ the totality of nodes being the branching points of tree; let $N_+(\omega)$ be the set of all nodes m being a member of $\mathcal{V} \setminus \mathcal{N}(\omega)$, whose direct predecessor lies in $\mathcal{N}(\omega)$ and which satisfies the condition $t_m(\omega) > 0$, and let $N_-(\omega)$ be the same set as described above but satisfying $t_m(\omega) \leqslant 0$. Finally, we put

$$N(\omega) = N_+(\omega) \cup N_-(\omega). \tag{10}$$

5. Star-product functional

This section treats a tree-based star-product functional. First of all, we denote by the symbol $\mathrm{Proj}^{z}(\cdot)$ a projection of the objective element onto its orthogonal part of the z component in $\mathbb{C}^3$, and we define a $\bigstar$-product of β, γ for $z \in D_0$ as

$$\beta \bigstar_{[z]} \gamma = -i(\beta \cdot e_z)\mathrm{Proj}^{z}(\gamma). \tag{11}$$

Notice that this product $\bigstar$ is noncommutative. This property will be the key point in defining the star-product functional below, especially as far as the uniqueness of functional is concerned. We shall define $\Theta^m(\omega)$ for each $\omega \in \Omega$ realized as follows. When $m \in N_+(\omega)$, then $\Theta^m(\omega) = \tilde{f}(t_m(\omega), x_m(\omega))$, while $\Theta^m(\omega) = u_0(x_m(\omega))$ if $m \in N_-(\omega)$. Then, we define

$$\Xi^{m_1}_{m_2.m_3}(\omega) \equiv \Xi^{m_1}_{m_2,m_3}[u_0,f](\omega) := \Theta^{m_2}(\omega) \bigstar_{[x_{m_1}]} \Theta^{m_3}(\omega), \tag{12}$$

whereas for the product order in the star-product $\bigstar$, when we write $m \prec m'$ lexicographically with respect to the natural order $\prec$, the term Θ^m labeled by m necessarily occupies the left-hand side, and the other $\Theta^{m'}$ labeled by m' occupies the right-hand side by all means. And besides, as abuse of notation, we write

$$\Xi^{\varnothing}_{m,\varnothing}(\omega) \equiv \Xi^{\varnothing}_{m,\varnothing}[u_0,f](\omega) := \Theta^m(\omega), \tag{13}$$

especially when $m \in \mathcal{V}$ is a label of single terminal point in the restricted tree structure in question.

Under these circumstances, we consider a random quantity which is obtained by executing the star-product $\bigstar$ inductively at each node in $\mathcal{N}(\omega)$, we call it a tree-based $\bigstar$-product functional, and we express it symbolically as

$$M_{\bigstar}{}^{\langle u_0,f\rangle}(\omega) = \Pi \bigstar_{[x_{\tilde{m}}]} \Xi^{m_1}_{m_2 \cdot m_3}[u_0,f](\omega), \tag{14}$$

where $m_1 \in \mathcal{N}(\omega)$ and $m_2, m_3 \in N(\omega)$, and by the symbol $\prod \bigstar$ (as a product relative to the star-product), we mean that the star-products $\bigstar$'s should be succeedingly executed in a lexicographical manner with respect to $x\tilde{m}$ such that $\tilde{m} \in \mathcal{N}(\omega) \cap \{|\tilde{m}| = \ell - 1\}$ when $|m_1| = \ell$. At any rate it is of the extreme importance that once a branching pattern $\omega(\in \Omega)$ is realized, its tree structure is uniquely determined, and there can be found the *unique* explicit representation of the corresponding star-product functional $M_{\bigstar}^{\langle u_0,f\rangle}(\omega)$.

Example 2. Let us consider a typical realization $\omega \in \Omega$. Suppose that we have $\mathcal{N}(\omega_2) = \{\phi, 1, 2, 11, 12, 22\}$, $N_+(\omega_2) = \{21, 112, 221\}$, and $N_-(\omega_2) = \{111, 121, 122, 222\}$. This case is nothing but an all-the-members participating type of game. For the case of particle located at x_{111} and x_{112} (with nodes of the level $|m| = \ell = 3$) with its pivoting node x_{11}, we have

$$\begin{aligned}\Xi^{11}_{111,112}(\omega_2) &= \Theta^{111}(\omega_2) \bigstar_{[x_{11}]} \Theta^{112}(\omega_2)\\ &= u_0(x_{111}(\omega_2)) \bigstar_{[x_{11}]} \tilde{f}(t_{112}(\omega_2), x_{112}(\omega_2)).\end{aligned}$$

Similarly, for the pair of particles x_{121} and x_{122}, we have

$$\begin{aligned}\Xi^{12}_{121,122}(\omega_2) &= \Theta^{121}(\omega_2) \bigstar_{[x_{12}]} \Theta^{122}(\omega_2)\\ &= u_0(x_{121}(\omega_2)) \bigstar_{[x_{12}]} u_0(x_{122}(\omega_2)).\end{aligned}$$

For the pair of particles x_{221} and x_{222}, we also have

$$\begin{aligned}\Xi^{22}_{221,222}(\omega_2) &= \Theta^{221}(\omega_2) \bigstar_{[x_{22}]} \Theta^{222}(\omega_2)\\ &= \tilde{f}(t_{221}(\omega_2), x_{221}(\omega_2)) \bigstar_{[x_{22}]} u_0(x_{222}(\omega_2)).\end{aligned}$$

Next, when we take a look at the groups of particles with nodes of the level $|m| = \ell = 2$. For instance, as to a pair of particles located at x_{11} and x_{12} with its pivoting node x_1, we get an expression

$$\begin{aligned}\Xi^{1}_{11,12}(\omega_2) &= \Theta^{11}(\omega_2) \bigstar_{[x_1]} \Theta^{12}(\omega_2)\\ &= \Xi^{11}_{111,112}(\omega_2) \bigstar_{[x_1]} \Xi^{12}_{121,122}(\omega_2)\\ &= \left(u_0(x_{111}) \bigstar_{[x_{11}]} \tilde{f}(t_{112}, x_{112})\right) \bigstar_{[x_1]} \left(u_0(x_{121}) \bigstar_{[x_{12}]} u_0(x_{122})\right).\end{aligned}$$

Therefore, it follows by a similar argument that the explicit representation of star-product functional for ω_2 is given by

$$M_{\bigstar}^{\langle u_0 f\rangle}(\omega_2)=\left\{\left(u_0(x_{111})\bigstar_{[x_{11}]}\tilde{f}(t_{112},x_{112})\right)\bigstar_{[x_1]}\left(u_0(x_{121})\bigstar_{[x_{12}]}u_0(x_{122})\right)\right\}$$
$$\bigstar_{[x_\phi]}\left\{\tilde{f}(t_{21},x_{21})\bigstar_{[x_2]}\left(u_0(x_{221})\bigstar_{[x_{22}]}u_0(x_{222})\right)\right\}$$

6. The *-product functional and existence

In this section we first begin with constructing a (U,F)-weighted tree-based *-product functional $M_*^{\langle U,F\rangle}(\omega)$, which is indexed by the nodes (x_m) of a binary tree. Recall that $U=U(x)$ (resp. $F=F(t,x)$) is a nonnegative measurable function on D_0 (resp. $\mathbb{R}_+\times D_0$), respectively, and also that $F(\cdot,x)\in L^1(\mathbb{R}_+)$ for each x. Moreover, in construction of the functional, the product is taken as ordinary multiplication * instead of the star-product $\bigstar$.

In what follows we shall give an outline of the existence in Theorem 1. We need the following lemma, which is essentially important for the proof.

Lemma 3. *For* $0\leqslant t\leqslant T$ *and* $x\in D_0$, *the function* $V(t,x)=E_{t,x}\left[M_*^{\langle U,F\rangle}(\omega)\right]$ *satisfies*

$$e^{\lambda t|x|^2}V(t,x)=U(x)+\int_0^t ds\frac{|x|^2}{2}e^{\lambda s|x|^2}\left\{F(s,x)+\int V(s,y)V(s,z)K_x(dy,z)\right\}. \quad (15)$$

Proof of Lemma 3. By making use of the conditional expectation, we may decompose $V(t,x)$ as follows:

$$\begin{aligned}V(t,x)&=E_{t,x}\left[M_*^{U,F}(\omega)\right]\\&=E_{t,x}\left[M_*^{\langle U,F\rangle}(\omega),\ t_\phi\leqslant 0\right]+E_{t,x}\left[M_*^{\langle U,F\rangle}(\omega),t_\phi>0\right]\\&=E_{t,x}\left[M_*^{U,F}(\omega),\ t_\phi\leqslant 0\right]+E_{t,x}\left[M_*^{\langle U,F\rangle}(\omega),t_\phi>0,\eta_\phi=0\right]\\&\quad+E_{t,x}\left[M_*^{\langle U,F\rangle}(\omega),\ t_\phi>0,\eta_\phi=1\right].\end{aligned} \quad (16)$$

We are next going to take into consideration an equivalence between the events $t_\phi\leqslant 0$ and $T\notin[0,t]$. Indeed, as to the first term in the third line of Eq. (16), since the condition $t_\phi\leqslant 0$ implies that T never lies in an interval $[0,t]$, and since $m=\phi\in N_-(\omega)$ leads to a nonrandom expression

$$M_*=\Theta^\phi=U(x),$$

the tree-based *-product functional is allowed to possess a simple representation:

$$\begin{aligned}E_{t,x}\left[M_*^{\langle U,F\rangle},t_\phi\leqslant 0\right]&=E_{t,x}\left[M_*^{\langle U,F\rangle}\cdot 1_{\{t_\phi\leqslant\leqslant 0\}}\right]=U(x)\cdot P_{t,x}(t_\phi\leqslant 0)\\&=U(x)\cdot P(T\notin[0,t])=U(x)\cdot P(T\in(t,\infty))\\&=U(x)\int_t^\infty f_T(s)ds=U(x)\int_t^\infty\lambda|x|^2e^{-\lambda s|x|^2}ds\\&=U(x)\cdot\exp\left\{-\lambda t|x|^2\right\}.\end{aligned} \quad (17)$$

As to the third term, we need to note the following matters. A particle generates two offsprings or descendants x_1,x_2 with probability $\frac{1}{2}$ under the condition $\eta_\phi=1$; since $t_\phi>0$, when the branching occurs at $t_\phi=s$, then, under the conditioning operation at t_ϕ, the Markov property [13] guarantees that the lower tree structure below the first-generation branching node point x_1 is independent to that below the location x_2 with realized $\omega \in \Omega$; hence, a tree-based $*$-product functional branched after time s is also probabilistically independent of the other tree-based $*$-product functional branched after time s, and besides the distributions of x_1 and x_2 are totally controlled by the Markov kernel K_x. Therefore, an easy computation provides with an impressive expression:

$$E_{t,x}\left[M_*^{\langle U,F\rangle}, t_\phi > 0, \eta_\phi = 1\right] = \frac{1}{2}\int_0^t \mathrm{d}s\,\lambda|x|^2 e^{-\lambda|x|^2(t-s)}.$$
$$\times \iint E_{s,x_1}[M_*]\cdot E_{s,x_2}[M_*]K_x(\mathrm{d}x_1, \mathrm{d}x_2).$$

Note that as for the second term, it goes almost similarly as the computation of the above-mentioned third one. Finally, summing up we obtain

$$\begin{aligned} V(t,x) &= E_{t,x}\left[M_*^{\langle U,F\rangle}(\omega)\right] \\ &= U(x)r^{-\lambda t|x|^2} + \int_0^t \frac{\lambda|x|^2}{2} e^{-\lambda|x|^2(t-s)}F(s,x)\,\mathrm{d}s \\ &\quad + \int_0^t \frac{\lambda|x|^2}{2} e^{-\lambda|x|^2(t-s)} \iint V(s,y)V(s,z)K_x(dy,dz)ds. \end{aligned} \tag{18}$$

On this account, if we multiply both sides of Eq. (18) by $\exp\left\{\lambda t|x|^2\right\}$, then the required expression Eq. (15) in Lemma 3 can be derived, which completes the proof. □

By a glance at the expression Eq. (15) obtained in Lemma 3, it is quite obvious that, for each $x \in D_0$, the mapping $[0,T]\ni t\mapsto e^{\lambda|x|^2 t}V(t,x) \in \overline{\mathbb{R}}_+$ is a nondecreasing function. Taking the above fact into consideration, we can deduce with ease that

$$E_{t,x}\left[M_*^{\langle U,F\rangle}(\omega)\right] < \infty \tag{19}$$

holds for $\forall t \in [0,T]$ and $x \in E_c$, where the measurable set E_c denotes the totality of all the elements x in D_0 such that $E_{T,x}\left[M_*^{\langle U,F\rangle}\right] < \infty$ holds for a.e.-x, namely, it is the same condition Eq. (7) appearing in the assertion of Theorem 1. Another important aspect for the proof consists in establishment of the M_*-control inequality, which is a basic property of the star-product $\bigstar$. That is to say, we have.

Lemma 4. (M_*-control inequality) *The following inequality*

$$|M_\bigstar^{\langle u_0,f\rangle}(\omega)| \leqslant M_*^{\langle U,F\rangle}(\omega). \tag{20}$$

holds $P_{t,x}$-a.s.

This inequality enables us to govern the behavior of the star-product functional with a very complicated structure by that of the $*$-product functional with a rather simplified structure. In fact, the M_*-control inequality yields immediately from a simple fact:

$$|w\bigstar_{[x]}v| \leqslant |w|\cdot|v| \quad \text{for every} \quad w, v \in \mathbb{C}^3 \quad \text{and every} \quad x \in D_0.$$

Next, we are going to derive the space of solutions to Eq. (2). If we define

$$u(t,x) := \begin{cases} E_{t,x}\left[M_\bigstar^{\langle u_0,f\rangle}(\omega)\right], & \text{on} \quad E_c, \\ 0, & \text{otherwise,} \end{cases}$$

then $u(t,x)$ is well defined on the whole space D_0 under the assumptions of the main theorem (Theorem 1). Moreover, it follows from the M_*-control inequality (Eq. (20)) that

$$|u(t,x)| \leqslant V(t,x) \quad \text{on} \quad [0,T] \times D_0. \tag{21}$$

On this account, from Eq. (15) in Lemma 3, by finiteness of the expectation of tree-based *-product functional $M_*^{\langle U,F\rangle}(\omega)$, by the M_*-control inequality, and from Eq. (21), it is easy to see that

$$\int_0^T \mathrm{d}s \int |u(s,y)| \cdot |u(s,z)| K_x(\mathrm{d}y,\mathrm{d}z) < \infty \qquad \text{for} \quad x \in E_c. \tag{22}$$

Hence, taking Eq. (22) into consideration, we define the space $\mathcal{D}$ of solutions to Eq. (2) as follows:

$$\begin{aligned} \mathcal{D} := \{ \varphi : \mathbb{R}_+ \times D_0 \to \mathbb{C}^3;\ \varphi \quad & \text{is continuous in} \quad t \\ \text{and measurable such that} & \\ \textstyle\int_0^\infty \mathrm{d}s \int e^{\lambda |x|^2 s} |\varphi(s,y)| \cdot |(s,z)| K_x(\mathrm{d}y,\mathrm{d}z) < \infty & \\ & \text{holds a.e.} - x \} \end{aligned} \tag{23}$$

By employing the Markov property [13] with respect to time t_ϕ and by a similar technique as in the proof of Lemma 3, we may proceed in rewriting and calculating the expectation for $\forall t > 0$ and $x \in E_c$:

$$\begin{aligned} u(t,x) &= E_{t,x}\left[M_\star^{\langle u_0 f\rangle}(\omega)\right] \\ &= E_{t,x}\left[M_\star^{\langle u_0 f\rangle}(\omega), t_\phi \leqslant 0\right] + E_{t,x}\left[M_\star^{\langle u_0 f\rangle}(\omega) t_\phi > 0\right] \\ &= E_{t,x}\left[M_\star^{\langle u_0 f\rangle}(\omega), t_\phi \leqslant 0\right] + E_{t,x}\left[M_\star^{\langle u_0 f\rangle}(\omega) t_\phi > 0, \eta_\phi = 0\right] \\ &\quad + E_{t,x}\left[M_\star^{\langle u_0 f\rangle}(\omega) t_\phi > 0\ \eta_\phi = 1\right] \\ &= e^{-t|x|^2} u_0(x) + \textstyle\int_0^t s\, |x|^2 e^{-(t-s)|x|^2} \\ &\quad \times \frac{1}{2}\left\{\tilde{f}(s,x) + \iint E_{s,x_1}[M_\star] \bigstar_{[x]} E_{s,x_2}[M_\star] K_x(\mathrm{d}x_1,\mathrm{d}x_2)\right\}. \end{aligned} \tag{24}$$

Furthermore, we may apply the integral equality Eq. (4) in the assumption on the Markov kernel for Eq. (24) to obtain

$$\begin{aligned} E_{t,x}\left[M_\star^{\langle u_0 f\rangle}(\omega)\right] &= e^{-\lambda t|x|^2} u_0(x) + \int_0^t \mathrm{d}s\, \lambda\, |x|^2 e^{-\lambda(t-s)|x|^2} \\ &\quad \times \frac{1}{2}\left\{\tilde{f}(s,x) + \iint E_{s,x_1}[M_\star] \bigstar_{[x]} E_{s,x_2}[M_\star] K_x(\mathrm{d}x_1,\mathrm{d}x_2)\right\} \\ &= e^{-\lambda t|x|^2} u_0(x) + \int_0^t \mathrm{d}s\, \lambda |x|^2 e^{-\lambda(t-s)|x|^2} \\ &\quad \times \frac{1}{2}\left\{\tilde{f}(s,x) + \iint u(s,y) \bigstar_{[x]} u(s,z) K_x(\mathrm{d}y,\mathrm{d}z)\right\} \\ &= e^{-\lambda t|x|^2}\left\{u_0(x) + \frac{\lambda}{2}\int_0^t e^{\lambda s|x|^2} f(s,x)\mathrm{d}s + \frac{\lambda}{2}\int_0^t \mathrm{d}s \int e^{\lambda s|x|^2} p(s,x,y;u) n(x,y)\mathrm{d}y\right\}, \end{aligned} \tag{25}$$

because in the above last equality we need to rewrite its double integral relative to the space parameters into a single integral. Finally, we attain that $u(t,x) = E_{t,x}\left[M_\star^{\langle u_0 f\rangle}(\omega)\right]$ satisfies the integral equation Eq. (2), and this $u(t,x)$ is a solution lying in the space $\mathcal{D}$. This completes the proof of the existence.

7. Uniqueness

First of all, note that we can choose a proper measurable subset $F_0 \subset D_0$ with $m(F_0^c) = m(D_0 \setminus F_0) = 0$ (meaning that its complement F_0^c is a null set with respect to Lebesgue measure $m(x)$), such that

$$E_{t,x}\left[M_*^{\langle U,F\rangle}(\omega)\right] < \infty \quad \text{on} \quad F_0 \tag{26}$$

and

$$\int_0^T \mathrm{d}s \iint e^{\lambda|x|^2 s}|u(s,y)| \cdot |u(s,z)|K_x(\mathrm{d}y, \mathrm{d}z), \quad \text{for} \quad \forall T > 0,$$

is convergent for a.e.-x $(\in F_0)$, and $u(t,x)$ satisfies the nonlinear integral equation (Eq. (2)) for a.e.-$x \in F_0$. Suggested by the argument in [7], we adopt here a martingale method in order to prove the uniqueness of the solutions to Eq. (2). The leading philosophy for the proof of uniqueness consists in extraction of the martingale part from the realized tree structure and in representation of the solution u in terms of martingale language. In so doing, we need to construct a martingale term from the given functional and to settle down the required σ-algebra with respect to which its constructed term may become a martingale. Let Ω_+ be the set of all the elements ω's corresponding to time $t_m(\omega) > 0$ for the label m. Next, we consider a kind of the notion like n-section of the set of labels for $n \in \mathbb{N}_0 := \mathbb{N} \cup \{0\}$. We define several families of Ω in what follows, in order to facilitate the extraction of its martingale part from our star-product functional $M_\star^{\langle u_0 f\rangle}(\omega)$. For each realized tree ω, $\tilde{\mathcal{N}}_n(\omega)$ is the totality of the labels

$$m \in \bigcup_{0 \leqslant \ell \leqslant n} \{1,2\}^\ell$$

satisfying $t_m(\omega) > 0$ and $\eta_m(\omega) = 1$. Namely, this family $\tilde{\mathcal{N}}_n(\omega)$ is a subset of labels restricted up to the nth generation and limited to the nodes related to branching at positive time. Moreover, let $\tilde{N}_n(\omega)$ be the set of labels lying in $\mathcal{N} \setminus \tilde{\mathcal{N}}_n(\omega)$ whose direct predecessor belongs to $\tilde{\mathcal{N}}_n(\omega)$. By convention, we define $\tilde{N}_n(\omega) = \{\varnothing\}$ if $\tilde{\mathcal{N}}_n(\omega) = \varnothing$. We shall introduce a new family $\tilde{N}_n^{cut}(\omega)$ of cutoff labels, which is determined by the set of labels $m \in \mathcal{V}$ whose direct predecessor belongs to $\tilde{\mathcal{N}}_n(\omega)$ and has length $|m| = n$, and we call this family $\tilde{N}_n^{cut}(\omega)$ the cutoff part of $\tilde{N}_n(\omega)$, while $\check{N}_n nct(\omega)$ is the non-cutoff part of $\tilde{N}_n(\omega)$, which is defined by

$$\check{N}_n nct(\omega) := \tilde{N}_n(\omega) \setminus \tilde{N}_n^{cut}(\omega). \tag{27}$$

We are now in a position to introduce a new class $M_\star^{n,\langle u_0 f,u\rangle}(\omega)$ of $\star$-product functional, which should be called the n-section of the star-product functional. In fact, by taking the above argument in Example 2 into account, we can define its

n-section as follows. In fact, if the label m is a member of the cutoff family $\tilde{N}_n^{cut}(\omega)$, the input data of the functional attached to m is given by $u(t_{p(m)}(\omega), x_m(\omega))$ instead of the usual initial data $u_0(x_m(\omega))$ or $\tilde{f}(t_m(\omega), x_m(\omega))$, where $p(m)$ indicates the direct ancestor m' of m having length n. On the other hand, if m lies in the non-cutoff family $\breve{N}_n nct(\omega)$, then the input data of the functional attached to m is completely the same as before with no change, that is, we use $u_0(x_m)$ if $t_m \leqslant 0$ and use $\tilde{f}(t_m, x_m)$ if $t_m > 0$. In such a way, we can construct a new $\bigstar$-product functional $M_\bigstar^{n,\langle u_0 f, u\rangle}(\omega)$ by the almost sure procedure, and we call it the n-section $\bigstar$-product functional. Similarly, we can also define the corresponding n-section $\bigstar$-product functional $M_*^{n,\langle U,F,V\rangle}(\omega)$. Simply enough, to get the *-product counterpart, we have only to replace those functions $u_0, \tilde{f}$ and u by U, F and V in the definition of $\bigstar$-product functional. As easily imagined, we can also derive an n-section version of M_*^n-control inequality:

Lemma 5. (M_*^n-control inequality) *The following inequality*

$$|M_\bigstar^{n,\langle u_0 f, u\rangle}(\omega)| \leqslant M_*^{n,\langle U,F,V\rangle}(\omega) \tag{28}$$

holds $P_{t,x}$-a.s.

because of the domination property: $|u(t,x)| \leqslant V(t,x)$ for $[0,T] \times D_0$, $|u_0(x)| \leqslant U(x)$ for $\forall x$, $|\tilde{f}(t,x)| \leqslant F(t,x)$ for $\forall t, x$, and a simple inequality $|w \bigstar_{[x]} v| \leqslant |w| \cdot |v|$ for $\forall w, v \in \mathbb{C}^3$ and $\forall x \in D_0$.

Let us now introduce a filtration $\{\mathcal{F}_n\}$ for $n \in \mathbb{N}_0$ on Ω_+, according to the discussion in Example 2. As a matter of fact, we define

$$\mathcal{F}_n := \sigma\left(\tilde{\mathcal{N}}_n(\omega); (t_m, x_m), m \in \tilde{\mathcal{N}}_n(\omega) \cup \breve{N}_n^{nct}(\omega); (\eta_m), m \in \tilde{N}_n^{cut}(\omega)\right) \tag{29}$$

for each $n \in \mathbb{N}_0$. Notice that $\tilde{\mathcal{N}}_n(\omega)$ itself determines the other two families $\tilde{N}_n^{cut}(\omega)$ and $\breve{N}_n nct(\omega)$. Then, it is readily observed that both functionals $M_\bigstar^{n,\langle u_0 f, u\rangle}(\omega)$ and $M_*^{n,\langle U,F,V\rangle}(\omega)$ are $\mathcal{F}_n$-adapted.

Lemma 6. *For each* $n \in \mathbb{N}_0$, *the equality*

$$M_*^{n,\langle U,F,V\rangle}(\omega) = E_{t,x}\left[M_*^{\langle U,F\rangle}(\omega) | \mathcal{F}_n\right] \tag{30}$$

holds $P_{t,x}$-a.s. *for every* $t \in [0,T]$ *and every* $x \in F_0$.

Proof. By its construction, we can conclude the equality of Eq. (30) from the strong Markov property [13] applied at times (t_m)s for $m \in \mathcal{V}$ of length n on the set $\left\{m \in \tilde{\mathcal{N}}_n(\omega)\right\} \in \mathcal{F}_n$. □

Moreover, an application of Lemma 6 with the n-section M_*^n-control inequality (Eq. (28)) shows the $P_{t,x}$-integrability of $M_\bigstar^{n,\langle u_0 f, u\rangle}(\omega)$ for every $t \in [0,T]$ and every $x \in F_0$. Actually, it proves to be true that a martingale part, in question, extracted by the star-product functional relative to those n-section families, is given by the n-section $\bigstar$-product functional $M_\bigstar^{n,\langle u_0 f, u\rangle}(\omega)$.

Lemma 7. The n-section $M_\bigstar^{n,\langle u_0 f, u\rangle}(\omega)$ of $\bigstar$-product functional with weight functions u_0 and f is an $\{\mathcal{F}_n\}$-martingale [8].

Proof. When we set $= E_{t,x}\left[M_\bigstar^n(\omega) | \mathcal{F}_n\right]$, then ξ_n turns out to be a $\{\mathcal{F}_n\}$-martingale, since

$$E_{t,x}[\xi_n | \mathcal{F}_{n-1}] = E_{t,x}\left[E_{t,x}\left[M_\bigstar^n | \mathcal{F}_n\right] | \mathcal{F}_{n-1}\right] = E_{t,x}\left[M_\bigstar^n|_{n-1}\right] = \xi_{n-1}$$

by virtue of the inclusion property of the σ-algebras. Consequently, it suffices to show that

$$E_{t,x}\left[M_{\star}^{\langle u_0 f\rangle}(\omega)|\mathcal{F}_n\right] = M_{\star}^{n,\,\langle u_0 f,u\rangle}(\omega) \tag{31}$$

holds a.s. By employing the representation formula (Eq. (8)), an conditioning argument leads to Eq. (31), because the establishment is verified by the Markov property applied at t_m and on the event $\left\{m \in \tilde{\mathcal{N}}_n\right\}$ being $\mathcal{F}_n$-measurable. □

Finally, the uniqueness yields from the following assertion.

Proposition 8. *When* $u(t,x)$ *is a solution to the nonlinear integral equation* (Eq. (2)), *then we have*

$$u(t,x) = E_{t,x}\left[M_{\star}^{\langle u_0 f\rangle}(\omega)\right] \tag{32}$$

holds for every $t \in [0,T]$ *and for* a.e.-x.

Proof. Our proof is technically due to a martingale method. We need the following lemma.

Lemma 9. *Let* $M_{\star}^{n,\,\langle u_0 f,u\rangle}(\omega)$ *be the n-section of* $\star$*-product functional, and let* $u(t,x)$ *be a solution of the nonlinear integral equation* (Eq. (2)). *Then, we have the following identity: for each* $n \in \mathbb{N}_0$

$$u(t,x) = E_{t,x}\left[M_{\star}^{n,\,\langle u_0 f,u\rangle}(\omega)\right] \tag{33}$$

holds for every t $(0 \leqslant t \leqslant T)$ *and every* $x \in F_0$.

Proof of Lemma 9. Recall that $M_{\star}^{n,\,\langle u_0 f,u\rangle}(\omega)$ is a martingale relative to $\{\mathcal{F}_n\}$. For $n = 0$, it follows from the identity (Eq. (31)) and by the martingale property that

$$\begin{aligned} E_{t,x}\left[M_{\star}^{0,\,\langle u_0 f,u\rangle}(\omega)\right] &= E_{t,x}\left[E_{t,x}\left[M_{\star}^{\langle u_0 f\rangle}(\omega)|\mathcal{F}_0\right]\right] \\ &= E_{t,x}\left[M_{\star}^{\langle u_0 f\rangle}(\omega)\right] = u(t,x). \end{aligned} \tag{34}$$

Next, for the case $n = 1$, by the same reason, we can get

$$\begin{aligned} E_{t,x}\left[M_{\star}^{1,\,\langle u_0 f,u\rangle}(\omega)\right] &= E_{t,x}\left[E_{t,x}\left[M_{\star}^{\langle u_0 f\rangle}(\omega)|\mathcal{F}_1\right]\right] \\ &= E_{t,x}\left[M_{\star}^{\langle u_0 f\rangle}(\omega)\right] = u(t,x). \end{aligned} \tag{35}$$

We resort to the mathematical induction with respect to $n \in \mathbb{N}_0$. If we assume the identity (Eq. (33)) for the case of n, then the case of $n+1$ reads at once

$$\begin{aligned} E_{t,x}\left[M_{\star}^{n+1,\,\langle u_0 f,u\rangle}(\omega)\right] &= E_{t,x}\left[E_{t,x}\left[M_{\star}^{n+1,\,\langle u_0 f,u\rangle}(\omega)|\mathcal{F}_n\right]\right] \\ &= E_{t,x}\left[M_{\star}^{n,\,\langle u_0 f,u\rangle}(\omega)\right] = u(t,x), \end{aligned} \tag{36}$$

where we made use of the martingale property in the first equality and employed the hypothesis of induction in the last identity. This concludes the assertion. □

To go back to the proof of Proposition 8. We define an $\mathcal{F}_n$-measurable event A_n as the set of $\omega \in \Omega_+$ such that $\tilde{\mathcal{N}}_n(\omega)$ contains some label m of length n. From the definition, it holds immediately that

$$M_\star^{\langle u_0 f\rangle}(\omega) = M_\star^{n,\langle u_0 f,u\rangle}(\omega) \quad \text{on} \quad \Omega_+ \ A_n. \tag{37}$$

Hence, for every $x \in F_0$ and $0 \leqslant t \leqslant T$ and $\forall n \in \mathbb{N}_0$, we may apply Lemma 9 for the expression below with the identity (Eq. (31)) to obtain

$$\begin{aligned}
&|u(t,x) - E_{t,x}\left[M_\star^{\langle u_0 f\rangle}(\omega)\right]| \\
&= |E_{t,x}\left[M_\star^{n,\langle u_0 f,u\rangle}(\omega)\right] - E_{t,x}\left[M_\star^{\langle u_0 f\rangle}(\omega)\right]| \\
&\leqslant |E_{t,x}\left[M_\star^{n,\langle u_0 f,u\rangle}(\omega) - M_\star^{\langle u_0 f\rangle}(\omega); A_n\right]| \\
&+|E_{t,x}\left[M_\star^{n,\langle u_0 f,u\rangle}(\omega) - M_\star^{\langle u_0 f\rangle}(\omega); A_n^c\right]| \\
&= |E_{t,x}\left[\left(M_\star^{n,\langle u_0 f,u\rangle}(\omega) - M_\star^{\langle u_0 f\rangle}(\omega)\right)\cdot 1_{A_n}\right]|
\end{aligned} \tag{38}$$

where the symbol $E_{t,x}[X(\omega);A]$ denotes the integral of $X(\omega)$ over a measurable event A with respect to the probability measure $P_{t,x}(d\omega)$, namely,

$$E_{t,x}[X(\omega);A] = E_{t,x}[X(\omega)\cdot 1_A] = \int_A X(\omega)P_{t,x}(d\omega).$$

Furthermore, we continue computing

$$\begin{aligned}
(38) &\leqslant |E_{t,x}\left[M_\star^{n,\langle u_0 f,u\rangle}(\omega)1_{A_n}\right]| + |E_{t,x}\left[M_\star^{\langle u_0 f\rangle}(\omega)1_{A_n}\right]| \\
&= |E_{t,x}\left[E_{t,x}\left[M_\star^{\langle u_0 f\rangle}(\omega)|\mathcal{F}_n\right]1_{A_n}\right]| + |E_{t,x}\left[M_\star^{\langle u_0 f\rangle}(\omega)1_{A_n}\right]| \\
&= 2|E_{t,x}\left[M_\star^{\langle u_0 f\rangle}(\omega)1_{A_n}\right]|.
\end{aligned} \tag{39}$$

Since $\cap_n A_n = \varnothing$ by the binary critical tree structure [12], and since we have an natural estimate

$$\begin{aligned}
&|M_\star^{\langle u_0 f\rangle}(\omega)1_{A_n}(\omega)| < M_\star^{\langle U,F\rangle}(\omega), \quad \text{a.s.} \\
&\text{and} \quad \lim_{n\to\infty} M_\star^{\langle u_0 f\rangle}(\omega)1_{A_n}(\omega) = 0, \quad \text{a.s.}
\end{aligned} \tag{40}$$

it follows by the bounded convergence theorem of Lebesgue that

$$\lim_{n\to\infty} |E_{t,x}\left[M_\star^{\langle u_0 f\rangle}(\omega)1_{A_n}\right]| = 0. \tag{41}$$

Consequently, from Eq. (39) and Eq. (41), we readily obtain

$$|u(t,x) - E_{t,x}\left[M_\star^{\langle u_0 f\rangle}(\omega)\right]| \to 0 \quad (\text{as} \quad n \to \infty) \tag{42}$$

holds for every $(t,x) \in [0,T] \times F_0$. Thus, we attain that $u(t,x) = E_{t,x}\left[M_\star^{\langle u_0 f\rangle}(\omega)\right]$, a.e.-$x \in F_0$. This finishes the proof of Proposition 8. □

Concurrently, this completes the proof of the uniqueness.

Acknowledgements

This work is supported in part by the Japan MEXT Grant-in-Aids SR(C) 17 K05358 and also by ISM Coop. Res. Program: 2011-CRP-5010.

Author details

Isamu Dôku
Department of Mathematics, Faculty of Education, Saitama University, Saitama, Japan

*Address all correspondence to: idoku@mail.saitama-u.ac.jp

References

[1] Dôku I. Star-product functional and unbiased estimator of solutions to nonlinear integral equations. Far East Journal of Mathematical Sciences. 2014; **89**:69-128

[2] Dôku I. On a limit theorem for environment-dependent models. Institute of Statistical Mathematics Research Reports. 2016;**352**:103-111

[3] Dôku I. A recursive inequality of empirical measures associated with EDM. Journal of Saitama University. Faculty of Education (Mathematics for Natural Science). 2016;**65**(2):253-259

[4] Dôku I. A support problem for superprocesses in terms of random measure. RIMS Kôkyûroku (Kyoto University). 2017;**2030**:108-115

[5] Dôku I. Exponential moments of solutions for nonlinear equations with catalytic noise and large deviation. Acta Applicandae Mathematicae. 2000;**63**: 101-117

[6] Dôku I. Removability of exceptional sets on the boundary for solutions to some nonlinear equations. Scientiae Mathematicae Japonicae. 2001;**54**: 161-169

[7] Le Jan Y, Sznitman AS. Stochastic cascades and 3-dimensional Navier-Stokes equations. Probability Theory and Related Fields. 1997;**109**:343-366

[8] Kallenberg O. Foundations of Modern Probability. 2nd ed. New York: Springer; 2002. 638 p

[9] Harris TE. The Theory of Branching Processes. Berlin: Springer-Verlag; 1963. 248 p

[10] Aldous D. Tree-based models for random distribution of mass. Journal of Statistical Physics. 1993;**73**:625-641

[11] Le Gall J-F. Random trees and applications. Probability Surveys. 2005; **2**:245-311

[12] Drmota M. Random Trees. Wien: Springer-Verlag; 2009. 458 p

[13] Dynkin EB. Markov Processes. Vol. 1. Berlin: Springer-Verlag; 1965. 380 p

Section 4

Computes Methods to Integral Equations and Their Integral Transforms

Chapter 4

Computation of Two-Dimensional Fourier Transforms for Noisy Band-Limited Signals

Weidong Chen

Abstract

The computation of the two-dimensional Fourier transform by the sampling points creates an ill-posed problem. In this chapter, we will cover this problem for the band-limited signals in the noisy case. We will present a regularized algorithm based on the two-dimensional Shannon Sampling Theorem, the two-dimensional Fourier series, and the regularization method. First, we prove the convergence property of the regularized solution according to the maximum norm. Then an error estimation is given according to the L^2-norm. The convergence property of the regularized Fourier series is given in theory, and some examples are given to compare the numerical results of the regularized Fourier series with the numerical results of the Fourier series.

Keywords: Fourier transform, band-limited signal, ill-posedness, regularization

AMS subject classifications: 65T40, 65R20, 65R30, 65R32

1. Introduction

The two-dimensional Fourier transform is widely applied in many fields [1–9]. In this chapter, the ill-posedness of the problem for computing two-dimensional Fourier transform is analyzed on a pair of spaces by the theory and examples in detail. A two-dimensional regularized Fourier series is presented with the proof of the convergence property and some experimental results.

First, we describe the band-limited signals.

Definition. For two positive $\Omega_1, \Omega_2 \in \mathbb{R}$, a function $f \in L^2(\mathbb{R}^2)$ is said to be band-limited if

$$\hat{f}(\omega_1, \omega_2) = 0, \forall(\omega_1, \omega_2) \in \mathbb{R}^2 \backslash [-\Omega_1, \Omega_1] \times [-\Omega_2, \Omega_2].$$

Here $\hat{f}$ is the Fourier transform of:

$$F(f)(\omega_1, \omega_2) = \hat{f}(\omega_1, \omega_2) = \int_{-\infty}^{\infty} \int_{-\infty}^{\infty} f(t_1, t_2) e^{it_1\omega_1 + it_2\omega_2} dt_1 dt_2, (\omega_1, \omega_2) \in \mathbb{R}^2. \quad (1)$$

We will consider the problem of computing $\hat{f}(\omega_1, \omega_2)$ from $f(t_1, t_2)$.

For band-limited signals, we have the following sampling theorem [4, 10, 11]. For the two-dimensional band-limited function above, we have

$$f(t_1, t_2) = \sum_{n_1=-\infty}^{\infty} \sum_{n_2=-\infty}^{\infty} f(n_1H_1, n_2H_2) \frac{\sin \Omega_1(t_1 - n_1H_1)}{\Omega_1(t_1 - n_1H_1)} \frac{\sin \Omega_2(t_2 - n_2H_2)}{\Omega_2(t_2 - n_2H_2)}, \quad (2)$$

where $H_1 := \pi/\Omega_1$ and $H_2 := \pi/\Omega_2$.

Calculating the Fourier transform of $f(t_1, t_2)$ by the formula (2), we have the formula which is same as the Fourier series

$$\hat{f}(\omega_1, \omega_2) = H_1H_2 \sum_{n_1=-\infty}^{\infty} \sum_{n_2=-\infty}^{\infty} f(n_1H_1, n_2H_2) e^{in_1H_1\omega_1 + in_2H_2\omega_2} P_\Omega(\omega_1, \omega_2), \quad (3)$$

where $P_\Omega(\omega_1, \omega_2) = 1_{[-\Omega_1,\Omega_1]\times[-\Omega_2,\Omega_2]}(\omega_1, \omega_2)$ is the characteristic function of $[-\Omega_1, \Omega_1] \times [-\Omega_2, \Omega_2]$.

In many practical problems, the samples $\{f(n_1H_1, n_2H_2)\}$ are noisy:

$$f(n_1H_1, n_2H_2) = f_T(n_1H_1, n_2H_2) + \eta(n_1H_1, n_2H_2), \quad (4)$$

where $\{\eta(n_1H_1, n_2H_2)\}$ is the noise

$$|\eta(n_1H_1, n_2H_2)| \le \delta, \quad (5)$$

and $f_T \in L^2$ is the exact band-limited signal.

The noise in the two-dimensional case is discussed in [5, 6], and the Tikhonov regularization method is used. However, there is too much computation in the Tikhonov regularization method since the solution of an Euler equation is required.

The ill-posedness in the one-dimensional case is considered in [12, 13]. The regularized Fourier series

$$\hat{f}_\alpha(\omega) = H \sum_{n=-\infty}^{\infty} \frac{f(nH)e^{inH\omega}}{1 + 2\pi\alpha + 2\pi\alpha(n_1H_1)^2} P_\Omega(\omega)$$

in [12] is given based on the regularized Fourier transform

$$F_\alpha[f] = \int_{-\infty}^{\infty} \frac{f(t)e^{i\omega t}dt}{1 + 2\pi\alpha + 2\pi\alpha t^2}$$

in [14]. The regularized Fourier transform was found by finding the minimizer of the Tikhonov's smoothing functional.

In this chapter, we will find a reliable algorithm for this ill-posed problem using a two-dimensional regularized Fourier series. In Section 2, the ill-posedness is discussed in the two-dimensional case. In Section 3, the regularized Fourier series and the proof of the convergence property are given. The bias and variance of regularized Fourier series are given in Section 4. The algorithm and the experimental results of numerical examples are given in Section 5. Finally, the conclusion is given in Section 6.

2. The ill-posedness

We will first study the ill-posedness of the problem (3) in the noisy case (4). The concept of ill-posed problems was introduced in [15]. Here we borrow the following definition from it.

Definition 2.1 Assume A: $D \to U$ is an operator in which D and U are metric spaces with distances $\rho_D(*, *)$ and $\rho_U(*, *)$, respectively. The problem

$$Az = u. \tag{6}$$

of determining a solution z in the space D from the "initial data" u in the space U is said to be well-posed on the pair of metric spaces (D, U) in the sense of Hadamard if the following three conditions are satisfied:

i. For every element $u \in U$, there exists a solution z in the space D; in other words, the mapping A is surjective.

ii. The solution is unique; in other words, the mapping A is injective.

iii. The problem is stable in the spaces (D, U): $\forall \in >0$, $\exists \delta>0$, such that

$$\rho_U(u_1, u_2) < \delta \Rightarrow \rho_D(z_1, z_2) < \in.$$

In other words, the inverse mapping A^{-1} is uniformly continuous. Problems that violate any of the three conditions are said to be ill-posed.

In this section, we discuss the ill-posedness of $A\hat{f} = f$ on the pair of Banach spaces $(L^2[-\Omega_1, \Omega_1] \times [-\Omega_2, \Omega_2], l^\infty(\mathbb{Z}^2))$, where $\hat{f}(\omega_1, \omega_2)$ is given by the Fourier series in Eq. (3).

The operator A in Eq. (6) is defined by the following formula:

$$A\hat{f} = f, \tag{7}$$

where $= \{f(n_1H_1, n_2H_2)\text{: } n_1 \in \mathbb{Z}, n_2 \in \mathbb{Z}\}$.

As usual, l^∞ is the space $\{a(n) : n \in \mathbb{Z}^2\}$ of bounded sequences. The norm of l^∞ is defined by

$$\|a\|_{l^\infty} = \sup_{n \in \mathbb{Z}^2} |a(n)|,$$

where

i. The existence condition is not satisfied.

ii. The uniqueness condition is satisfied.

iii. The stability condition is not satisfied. The proof is similar to the proof in [10].

3. The regularized Fourier series

Based on the one-dimensional regularized Fourier series in [12], we construct the two-dimensional regularized Fourier series:

$$\hat{f}_\alpha(\omega_1, \omega_2) = H_1 H_2 \sum_{n_1=-\infty}^{\infty} \sum_{n_2=-\infty}^{\infty} \frac{f(n_1H_1, n_2H_2) e^{in_1H_1\omega_1 + in_2H_2\omega_2}}{\left[1 + 2\pi\alpha + 2\pi\alpha(n_1H_1)^2\right]\left[1 + 2\pi\alpha + 2\pi\alpha(n_2H_2)^2\right]} P_\Omega(\omega_1, \omega_2), \tag{8}$$

where $f(n_1H_1, n_2H_2)$ is given in (4). We will give the convergence property of the regularized Fourier series in this section.

Lemma 3.1

$$F\left[\frac{1}{1+2\pi\alpha+2\pi\alpha t^2}\frac{\sin\Omega(t-nH)}{\Omega(t-nH)}\right]=\frac{H}{1+2\pi\alpha+2\pi\alpha(nH)^2}e^{inH\omega}-\frac{H}{4\pi a\alpha}(-1)^n\left[\frac{e^{a(\omega-\Omega)}}{a-inH}+\frac{e^{-a(\omega+\Omega)}}{a+inH}\right], \tag{9}$$

where $a:=\sqrt{\frac{1+2\pi\alpha}{2\pi\alpha}}$.

Proof.

$$F\left[\frac{1}{1+2\pi\alpha+2\pi\alpha t^2}\frac{\sin\Omega(t-nH)}{\Omega(t-nH)}\right]=\frac{1}{2\pi}F\left[\frac{1}{1+2\pi\alpha+2\pi\alpha t^2}\right]*F\left[\frac{\sin\Omega(t-nH)}{\Omega(t-nH)}\right]$$

$$=\frac{1}{2\pi}\frac{1}{2a\alpha}e^{-a|\omega|}*\left[He^{i\omega nH}P_\Omega(\omega)\right]=H\frac{1}{4\pi a\alpha}\int_{-\infty}^{\infty}e^{-a|u|}e^{inH(\omega-u)}1_{[\omega-\Omega,\omega+\Omega]}(u)du$$

$$=H\frac{1}{4\pi a\alpha}e^{inH\omega}\int_{\omega-\Omega}^{\omega+\Omega}e^{-a|u|-inHu}du=H\frac{1}{4\pi a\alpha}e^{inH\omega}\left(\int_{\omega-\Omega}^{0}e^{au-inHu}du+\int_{0}^{\omega+\Omega}e^{-au-inHu}du\right)$$

$$=H\frac{1}{4\pi a\alpha}e^{inH\omega}\left[\frac{1}{a-inH}-\frac{e^{(a-inH)(\omega-\Omega)}}{a-inH}+\frac{1}{a+inH}-\frac{e^{-(a+inH)(\omega+\Omega)}}{a+inH}\right]$$

$$=H\frac{1}{4\pi a\alpha}e^{inH\omega}\left(\frac{1}{a-inH}+\frac{1}{a+inH}\right)-H\frac{1}{4\pi a\alpha}e^{inH\omega}\left[\frac{e^{(a-inH)(\omega-\Omega)}}{a-inH}+\frac{e^{-(a+inH)(\omega+\Omega)}}{a+inH}\right]$$

$$=H\frac{1}{2\pi\alpha}\frac{e^{inH\omega}}{a^2+(nH)^2}-H\frac{1}{4\pi a\alpha}e^{inH\omega}(-1)^n\left[\frac{e^{a(\omega-\Omega)-inH\omega}}{a-inH}+\frac{e^{-a(\omega+\Omega)-inH\omega}}{a+inH}\right]$$

$$=H\frac{e^{inH\omega}}{1+2\pi\alpha+2\pi\alpha(nH)^2}-H\frac{1}{4\pi a\alpha}(-1)^n\left[\frac{e^{a(\omega-\Omega)}}{a-inH}+\frac{e^{-a(\omega+\Omega)}}{a+inH}\right].$$

Lemma 3.2 For any band-limited function $g(t_1,t_2)$ and $(\omega_1,\omega_2)\in[-\Omega_1,\Omega_1]\times[-\Omega_2,\Omega_2]$

$$\int_{-\infty}^{\infty}\int_{-\infty}^{\infty}\frac{g(t_1,t_2)e^{it_1\omega_1+it_2\omega_2}dt_1dt_2}{(1+2\pi\alpha+2\pi\alpha t_1^2)(1+2\pi\alpha+2\pi\alpha t_2^2)}$$

$$=H_1H_2\sum_{n_1=-\infty}^{\infty}\sum_{n_2=-\infty}^{\infty}g(n_1H_1,n_2H_2)\frac{e^{in_1H_1\omega_1+in_2H_2\omega_2}}{[1+2\pi\alpha+2\pi\alpha(n_1H_1)^2][1+2\pi\alpha+2\pi\alpha(n_2H_2)^2]}$$

$$-H_1H_2\sum_{n_1=-\infty}^{\infty}\sum_{n_2=-\infty}^{\infty}g(n_1H_1,n_2H_2)\left[\frac{e^{in_1H_1\omega_1}}{1+2\pi\alpha+2\pi\alpha(n_1H_1)^2}\frac{(-1)^{n_2}}{4\pi a\alpha}\left(\frac{e^{a(\omega_2-\Omega_2)}}{a-in_2H_2}+\frac{e^{-a(\omega_2+\Omega_2)}}{a+in_2H_2}\right)\right]$$

$$-H_1H_2\sum_{n_1=-\infty}^{\infty}\sum_{n_2=-\infty}^{\infty}g(n_1H_1,n_2H_2)\left[\frac{e^{in_2H_2\omega_2}}{1+2\pi\alpha+2\pi\alpha(n_2H_2)^2}\frac{(-1)^{n_1}}{4\pi a\alpha}\left(\frac{e^{a(\omega_1-\Omega_1)}}{a-in_1H_1}+\frac{e^{-a(\omega_1+\Omega_1)}}{a+in_1H_1}\right)\right]$$

$$+H_1H_2\sum_{n_1=-\infty}^{\infty}\sum_{n_2=-\infty}^{\infty}g(n_1H_1,n_2H_2)\frac{(-1)^{n_1+n_2}}{(4\pi a\alpha)^2}\left[\frac{e^{a(\omega_1-\Omega_1)}}{a-in_1H_1}+\frac{e^{-a(\omega_1+\Omega_1)}}{a+in_1H_1}\right]\cdot\left[\frac{e^{a(\omega_2-\Omega_2)}}{a-in_2H_2}+\frac{e^{-a(\omega_2+\Omega_2)}}{a+in_2H_2}\right]. \tag{10}$$

Proof. By the sampling theorem

$$I := \int_{-\infty}^{\infty}\int_{-\infty}^{\infty} \frac{g(t_1,t_2)e^{it_1\omega_1+it_2\omega_2}dt_1dt_2}{(1+2\pi\alpha+2\pi\alpha t_1^2)(1+2\pi\alpha+2\pi\alpha t_2^2)}$$

$$= \int_{-\infty}^{\infty}\int_{-\infty}^{\infty} \frac{e^{it_1\omega_1+it_2\omega_2}}{(1+2\pi\alpha+2\pi\alpha t_1^2)(1+2\pi\alpha+2\pi\alpha t_2^2)} \cdot \sum_{n_1=-\infty}^{\infty}\sum_{n_2=-\infty}^{\infty} g(n_1H_1,n_2H_2)\frac{\sin\Omega_1(t_1-n_1H_1)}{\Omega_1(t_1-n_1H_1)}\frac{\sin\Omega_2(t_2-n_2H_2)}{\Omega_2(t_2-n_2H_2)}dt_1dt_2$$

$$= \sum_{n_1=-\infty}^{\infty}\sum_{n_2=-\infty}^{\infty} g(n_1H_1,n_2H_2)\int_{-\infty}^{\infty}\frac{1}{1+2\pi\alpha+2\pi\alpha t_1^2}\frac{\sin\Omega_1(t_1-n_1H_1)}{\Omega_1(t_1-n_1H_1)}e^{it_1\omega_1}dt_1 \cdot \int_{-\infty}^{\infty}\frac{1}{1+2\pi\alpha+2\pi\alpha t_2^2}\frac{\sin\Omega_2(t_2-n_2H_2)}{\Omega_2(t_2-n_2H_2)}e^{it_2\omega_2}dt_2$$

By Lemma 3.1 and the FOIL method, Eq. (10) is true.

Lemma 3.3 For each arbitrarily small $c>0$ and $\omega\in[-\Omega+c,\Omega-c]$,

$$\sum_{n=-\infty}^{\infty}\left|\frac{e^{a(\omega-\Omega)}}{a-inH}+\frac{e^{-a(\omega+\Omega)}}{a+inH}\right|^2 = O\left(\frac{e^{-2ac}}{a}\right). \tag{11}$$

Proof. By the inequality $|a+b|^2\le 2(|a|^2+|b|^2)$,

$$\sum_{n=-\infty}^{\infty}\left|\frac{e^{a(\omega-\Omega)}}{a-inH}+\frac{e^{-a(\omega+\Omega)}}{a+inH}\right|^2 \le 2\sum_{n=-\infty}^{\infty}\left[\left|\frac{e^{a(\omega-\Omega)}}{a-inH}\right|^2+\left|\frac{e^{-a(\omega+\Omega)}}{a+inH}\right|^2\right]$$

$$\le 4\sum_{n=-\infty}^{\infty}\frac{e^{-2ac}}{a^2+(nH)^2}\le\frac{4}{H}e^{-2ac}\int_{-\infty}^{\infty}\frac{dx}{a^2+x^2}+\frac{4}{a^2}e^{-2ac}=\frac{4\pi e^{-2ac}}{Ha}+\frac{4}{a^2}e^{-2ac}.$$

Lemma 3.4 For each arbitrarily small $c>0$ and $(\omega_1,\omega_2)\in[-\Omega_1+c,\Omega_1-c]\times[-\Omega_2+c,\Omega_2-c]$,

$$\sum_{n_1=-\infty}^{\infty}\sum_{n_2=-\infty}^{\infty} g(n_1H_1,n_2H_2)\frac{(-1)^{n_1+n_2}}{(4\pi a\alpha)^2}\left[\frac{e^{a(\omega_1-\Omega_1)}}{a-in_1H_1}+\frac{e^{-a(\omega_1+\Omega_1)}}{a+in_1H_1}\right] \left[\frac{e^{a(\omega_2-\Omega_2)}}{a-in_2H_2}+\frac{e^{-a(\omega_2+\Omega_2)}}{a+in_2H_2}\right], = O(ae^{-2ac}). \tag{12}$$

for $\alpha\to+0$ and g that is Ω-band-limited.

Proof. By the Cauchy inequality,

$$\left|\sum_{n_1=-\infty}^{\infty}\sum_{n_2=-\infty}^{\infty} g(n_1H_1,n_2H_2)\left[\frac{e^{a(\omega_1-\Omega_1)}}{a-in_1H_1}+\frac{e^{-a(\omega_1+\Omega_1)}}{a+in_1H_1}\right]\left[\frac{e^{a(\omega_2-\Omega_2)}}{a-in_2H_2}+\frac{e^{-a(\omega_2+\Omega_2)}}{a+in_2H_2}\right]\right|^2$$

$$\le \sum_{n_1=-\infty}^{\infty}\sum_{n_2=-\infty}^{\infty}|g(n_1H_1,n_2H_2)|^2$$

$$\sum_{n_1=-\infty}^{\infty}\sum_{n_2=-\infty}^{\infty}\left|\left[\frac{e^{a(\omega_1-\Omega_1)}}{a-in_1H_1}+\frac{e^{-a(\omega_1+\Omega_1)}}{a+in_1H_1}\right]\left[\frac{e^{a(\omega_2-\Omega_2)}}{a-in_2H_2}+\frac{e^{-a(\omega_2+\Omega_2)}}{a+in_2H_2}\right]\right|^2,$$

where $\sum_{n_1=-\infty}^{\infty}\sum_{n_2=-\infty}^{\infty}|g(n_1H_1, n_2H_2)|^2$ is bounded by Parseval equality, and

$$\sum_{n_1=-\infty}^{\infty}\sum_{n_2=-\infty}^{\infty}\left|\left[\frac{e^{a(\omega_1-\Omega_1)}}{a-in_1H_1}+\frac{e^{-a(\omega_1+\Omega_1)}}{a+in_1H_1}\right]\left[\frac{e^{a(\omega_2-\Omega_2)}}{a-in_2H_2}+\frac{e^{-a(\omega_2+\Omega_2)}}{a+in_2H_2}\right]\right|^2$$

$$=\sum_{n_1=-\infty}^{\infty}\left|\left[\frac{e^{a(\omega_1-\Omega_1)}}{a-in_1H_1}+\frac{e^{-a(\omega_1+\Omega_1)}}{a+in_1H_1}\right]\right|^2\sum_{n_2=-\infty}^{\infty}\left|\left[\frac{e^{a(\omega_1-\Omega_1)}}{a-in_1H_1}+\frac{e^{-a(\omega_1+\Omega_1)}}{a+in_1H_1}\right]\right|^2.$$

By Lemma 3.3, Eq. (12) is true.

Lemma 3.5

$$\sum_{n=-\infty}^{\infty}\left|\frac{1}{1+2\pi\alpha+2\pi\alpha(nH)^2}\right|^2=O\left(\frac{1}{\sqrt{\alpha}}\right). \tag{13}$$

Proof.

$$\sum_{n=-\infty}^{\infty}\left|\frac{1}{1+2\pi\alpha+2\pi\alpha(nH)^2}\right|^2\le\left|\frac{1}{1+2\pi\alpha}\right|^2+\sum_{n\neq0}\left|\frac{1}{1+2\pi\alpha+2\pi\alpha(nH)^2}\right|^2,$$

where

$$\sum_{n\neq0}\left|\frac{1}{1+2\pi\alpha+2\pi\alpha(nH)^2}\right|^2\le2\sum_{n=1}^{\infty}\frac{1}{\left[1+2\pi\alpha+2\pi\alpha(nH)^2\right]^2}\le$$

$$\frac{2}{H}\int_0^{\infty}\frac{dx}{(1+2\pi\alpha+2\pi\alpha x^2)^2}=O\left(\frac{1}{\sqrt{\alpha}}\right).$$

So

$$\sum_{n=-\infty}^{\infty}\left|\frac{1}{1+2\pi\alpha+2\pi\alpha(nH)^2}\right|^2=O\left(\frac{1}{\sqrt{\alpha}}\right).$$

Lemma 3.6 For each arbitrarily small $c>0$ and $(\omega_1,\omega_2)\in[-\Omega_1+c,\Omega_1-c]\times[-\Omega_2+c,\Omega_2-c]$,

$$\sum_{n_1=-\infty}^{\infty}\sum_{n_2=-\infty}^{\infty}g(n_1H_1,n_2H_2)\left[\frac{e^{in_1H_1\omega_1}}{1+2\pi\alpha+2\pi\alpha(n_1H_1)^2}\frac{(-1)^{n_2}}{4\pi a\alpha}\left(\frac{e^{a(\omega_2-\Omega_2)}}{a-in_2H_2}+\frac{e^{-a(\omega_2+\Omega_2)}}{a+in_2H_2}\right)\right]$$
$$=O\left(a^{\frac{1}{2}}e^{-ac}\right), \tag{14}$$

for $\alpha\to+0$ and g that is Ω-band-limited.

Proof. By Cauchy inequality,

$$\left|\sum_{n_1=-\infty}^{\infty}\sum_{n_2=-\infty}^{\infty}g(n_1H_1,n_2H_2)\left[\frac{e^{in_1H_1\omega_1}}{1+2\pi\alpha+2\pi\alpha(n_1H_1)^2}\right]\left[\frac{e^{a(\omega_2-\Omega_2)}}{a-in_2H_2}+\frac{e^{-a(\omega_2+\Omega_2)}}{a+in_2H_2}\right]\right|^2$$

$$\le\sum_{n_1=-\infty}^{\infty}\sum_{n_2=-\infty}^{\infty}|g(n_1H_1,n_2H_2)|^2$$

$$\sum_{n_1=-\infty}^{\infty}\sum_{n_2=-\infty}^{\infty}\left|\left[\frac{e^{in_1H_1\omega_1}}{1+2\pi\alpha+2\pi\alpha(n_1H_1)^2}\right]\left[\frac{e^{a(\omega_2-\Omega_2)}}{a-in_2H_2}+\frac{e^{-a(\omega_2+\Omega_2)}}{a+in_2H_2}\right]\right|^2,$$

where $\sum_{n_1=-\infty}^{\infty}\sum_{n_2=-\infty}^{\infty}|g(n_1H_1,n_2H_2)|^2$ is bounded by the Parseval equality, and

$$\sum_{n_1=-\infty}^{\infty}\sum_{n_2=-\infty}^{\infty}\left|\left[\frac{e^{in_1H_1\omega_1}}{1+2\pi\alpha+2\pi\alpha(n_1H_1)^2}\right]\left[\frac{e^{a(\omega_2-\Omega_2)}}{a-in_2H_2}+\frac{e^{-a(\omega_2+\Omega_2)}}{a+in_2H_2}\right]\right|^2$$
$$=\sum_{n_1=-\infty}^{\infty}\left|\frac{e^{in_1H_1\omega_1}}{1+2\pi\alpha+2\pi\alpha(n_1H_1)^2}\right|^2\sum_{n_2=-\infty}^{\infty}\left|\left[\frac{e^{a(\omega_2-\Omega_2)}}{a-in_2H_2}+\frac{e^{-a(\omega_2+\Omega_2)}}{a+in_2H_2}\right]\right|^2.$$

By Lemma 3.3 and Lemma 3.5 Eq. (14) is true.
Lemma 3.7

$$\sum_{n_1=-\infty}^{\infty}\sum_{n_2=-\infty}^{\infty}\left|\frac{\eta(n_1H_1,n_2H_2)}{[1+2\pi\alpha+2\pi\alpha(n_1H_1)^2][1+2\pi\alpha+2\pi\alpha(n_2H_2)^2]}\right|=O\left(\frac{\delta}{\alpha}\right) \tag{15}$$

for $\delta\to+0$ and $\alpha\to+0$, where η and δ are given in (4) and (5) in Section 1.
Proof.

$$\sum_{n=-\infty}^{\infty}\left|\frac{1}{1+2\pi\alpha+2\pi\alpha(nH_1)^2}\right|\le\left|\frac{1}{1+2\pi\alpha}\right|+\sum_{n\neq 0}\left|\frac{1}{1+2\pi\alpha+2\pi\alpha(nH_1)^2}\right|,$$

where

$$\sum_{n\neq 0}\left|\frac{1}{1+2\pi\alpha+2\pi\alpha(nH_1)^2}\right|\le 2\sum_{n=1}^{\infty}\frac{1}{1+2\pi\alpha+2\pi\alpha(nH_1)^2}$$
$$\le\frac{2}{H_1}\int_0^{\infty}\frac{dx}{1+2\pi\alpha+2\pi\alpha x^2}=O\left(\frac{1}{\sqrt{\alpha}}\right).$$

So

$$\sum_{n=-\infty}^{\infty}\left|\frac{1}{1+2\pi\alpha+2\pi\alpha(nH_1)^2}\right|=O(1/\sqrt{\alpha}).$$

For the same reason,

$$\sum_{n=-\infty}^{\infty}\left|\frac{1}{1+2\pi\alpha+2\pi\alpha(nH_2)^2}\right|=O\left(\frac{1}{\sqrt{\alpha}}\right).$$

So Eq. (15) is true.

Theorem 3.1 Suppose $f_T\in L^1(\mathbb{R}^2)\cap L^2(\mathbb{R}^2)$ is band-limited. For each arbitrarily small $c>0$, if we choose $\alpha=\alpha(\delta)$ such that $\alpha(\delta)\to 0$ and $\delta/\alpha(\delta)\to 0$ as $\delta\to 0$, then $\hat{f}_\alpha(\omega_1,\omega_2)\to\hat{f}_T(\omega_1,\omega_2)$ uniformly in $(\omega_1,\omega_2)\in[-\Omega_1+c,\Omega_1-c]\times[-\Omega_2+c,\Omega_2-c]$ as $\delta\to 0$.
Proof. By Lemma 3.2, Lemma 3.4 and Lemma 3.6, we have

$$H_1H_2\sum_{n_1=-\infty}^{\infty}\sum_{n_2=-\infty}^{\infty}\frac{f_T(n_1H_1,n_2H_2)}{[1+2\pi\alpha+2\pi\alpha(n_1H_1)^2][1+2\pi\alpha+2\pi\alpha(n_2H_2)^2]}e^{in_1H_1\omega_1+in_2H_2\omega_2}$$
$$=\int_{-\infty}^{\infty}\int_{-\infty}^{\infty}\frac{f_T(t_1,t_2)e^{it_1\omega_1+it_2\omega_2}dt_1dt_2}{(1+2\pi\alpha+2\pi\alpha t_1^2)(1+2\pi\alpha+2\pi\alpha t_2^2)}+O\left(a^{\frac{1}{2}}e^{-ac}\right).$$

Therefore,

$$\hat{f}_a(\omega_1,\omega_2)-\hat{f}_T(\omega_1,\omega_2)=H_1H_2\sum_{n_1=-\infty}^{\infty}\sum_{n_2=-\infty}^{\infty}\frac{[f_T(n_1H_1,n_2H_2)+\eta(n_1H_1,n_2H_2)]e^{in_1H_1\omega_1+in_2H_2\omega_2}}{[1+2\pi\alpha+2\pi\alpha(n_1H_1)^2][1+2\pi\alpha+2\pi\alpha(n_2H_2)^2]}P_\Omega(\omega_1,\omega_2)-\hat{f}_T(\omega_1,\omega_2)$$

$$=H_1H_2\sum_{n_1=-\infty}^{\infty}\sum_{n_2=-\infty}^{\infty}\frac{f_T(n_1H_1,n_2H_2)e^{in_1H_1\omega_1+in_2H_2\omega_2}}{[1+2\pi\alpha+2\pi\alpha(n_1H_1)^2][1+2\pi\alpha+2\pi\alpha(n_2H_2)^2]}P_\Omega(\omega_1,\omega_2)-\hat{f}_T(\omega_1,\omega_2)$$

$$+H_1H_2\sum_{n_1=-\infty}^{\infty}\sum_{n_2=-\infty}^{\infty}\frac{\eta(n_1H_1,n_2H_2)}{[1+2\pi\alpha+2\pi\alpha(n_1H_1)^2][1+2\pi\alpha+2\pi\alpha(n_2H_2)^2]}e^{in_1H_1\omega_1+in_2H_2\omega_2}P_\Omega(\omega_1,\omega_2)$$

$$=\left[\int_{-\infty}^{\infty}\int_{-\infty}^{\infty}\frac{f_T(t_1,t_2)e^{it_1\omega_1+it_2\omega_2}dt_1dt_2}{(1+2\pi\alpha+2\pi\alpha t_1^2)(1+2\pi\alpha+2\pi\alpha t_2^2)}-\int_{-\infty}^{\infty}\int_{-\infty}^{\infty}f_T(t_1,t_2)e^{it_1\omega_1+it_2\omega_2}dt_1dt_2\right]P_\Omega(\omega_1,\omega_2)$$

$$+H_1H_2\sum_{n_1=-\infty}^{\infty}\sum_{n_2=-\infty}^{\infty}\frac{\eta(n_1H_1,n_2H_2)e^{in_1H_1\omega_1+in_2H_2\omega_2}}{\left[1+2\pi\alpha+2\pi\alpha(n_1H_1)^2\right]\left[1+2\pi\alpha+2\pi\alpha(n_2H_2)^2\right]}P_\Omega(\omega_1,\omega_2)+O\left(a^{\frac{1}{2}}e^{-ac}\right).$$

This implies

$$\left|\hat{f}_a(\omega_1,\omega_2)-\hat{f}_T(\omega_1,\omega_2)\right|$$

$$\leq\left|\int_{-\infty}^{\infty}\int_{-\infty}^{\infty}\frac{4\pi\alpha+2\pi\alpha t_1^2+2\pi\alpha t_2^2+(2\pi\alpha+2\pi\alpha t_1^2)(2\pi\alpha+2\pi\alpha t_2^2)}{(1+2\pi\alpha+2\pi\alpha t_1^2)(1+2\pi\alpha+2\pi\alpha t_2^2)}f_T(t_1,t_2)e^{it_1\omega_1+it_2\omega_2}dt_1dt_2\right|$$

$$+H_1H_2\left|\sum_{n_1=-\infty}^{\infty}\sum_{n_2=-\infty}^{\infty}\frac{\eta(n_1H_1,n_2H_2)}{[1+2\pi\alpha+2\pi\alpha(n_1H_1)^2][1+2\pi\alpha+2\pi\alpha(n_2H_2)^2]}e^{in_1H_1\omega_1+in_2H_2\omega_2}\right|$$

$$+O\left(a^{\frac{1}{2}}e^{-ac}\right)$$

where

$$\left|\sum_{n_1=-\infty}^{\infty}\sum_{n_2=-\infty}^{\infty}\frac{\eta(n_1H_1,n_2H_2)}{\left[1+2\pi\alpha+2\pi\alpha(n_1H_1)^2\right]\left[1+2\pi\alpha+2\pi\alpha(n_2H_2)^2\right]}e^{in_1H_1\omega_1+in_2H_2\omega_2}\right|=O\left(\frac{\delta}{\alpha}\right).$$

For any $\varepsilon>0$, there exists $M>0$ such that

$$\iint_{|t_1|\geq M\ or\ |t_2|\geq M}\left|f_T(t_1,t_2)\right|dt_1dt_2<\varepsilon.$$

Then

$$\left|\int_{-\infty}^{\infty}\int_{-\infty}^{\infty}\frac{4\pi\alpha+2\pi\alpha t_1^2+2\pi\alpha t_2^2+(2\pi\alpha+2\pi\alpha t_1^2)(2\pi\alpha+2\pi\alpha t_2^2)}{(1+2\pi\alpha+2\pi\alpha t_1^2)(1+2\pi\alpha+2\pi\alpha t_2^2)}f_T(t_1,t_2)e^{it_1\omega_1+it_2\omega_2}dt_1dt_2\right|$$

$$\leq\left|\iint_{|t_1|\leq M\ and\ |t_2|\leq M}\frac{4\pi\alpha+2\pi\alpha t_1^2+2\pi\alpha t_2^2+(2\pi\alpha+2\pi\alpha t_1^2)(2\pi\alpha+2\pi\alpha t_2^2)}{(1+2\pi\alpha+2\pi\alpha t_1^2)(1+2\pi\alpha+2\pi\alpha t_2^2)}f_T(t_1,t_2)e^{it_1\omega_1+it_2\omega_2}dt_1dt_2\right|$$

$$+\left|\iint_{|t_1|\geq M\ or\ |t_2|\geq M}\frac{4\pi\alpha+2\pi\alpha t_1^2+2\pi\alpha t_2^2+(2\pi\alpha+2\pi\alpha t_1^2)(2\pi\alpha+2\pi\alpha t_2^2)}{(1+2\pi\alpha+2\pi\alpha t_1^2)(1+2\pi\alpha+2\pi\alpha t_2^2)}f_T(t_1,t_2)e^{it_1\omega_1+it_2\omega_2}dt_1dt_2\right|,$$

where

$$\left| \iint\limits_{|t_1|\geq M \ or \ |t_2|\geq M} \frac{4\pi\alpha + 2\pi\alpha t_1^2 + 2\pi\alpha t_2^2 + \left(2\pi\alpha + 2\pi\alpha t_1^2\right)\left(2\pi\alpha + 2\pi\alpha t_2^2\right)}{\left(1 + 2\pi\alpha + 2\pi\alpha t_1^2\right)\left(1 + 2\pi\alpha + 2\pi\alpha t_2^2\right)} f_T(t_1, t_2) e^{it_1\omega_1 + it_2\omega_2} dt_1 dt_2 \right|$$

$$\leq \iint\limits_{|t_1|\geq M \ or \ |t_2|\geq M} |f_T(t_1, t_2)| dt_1 dt_2 < \varepsilon$$

and

$$\left| \iint\limits_{|t_1|\leq M \ and \ |t_2|\leq M} \frac{4\pi\alpha + 2\pi\alpha t_1^2 + 2\pi\alpha t_2^2 + \left(2\pi\alpha + 2\pi\alpha t_1^2\right)\left(2\pi\alpha + 2\pi\alpha t_2^2\right)}{\left(1 + 2\pi\alpha + 2\pi\alpha t_1^2\right)\left(1 + 2\pi\alpha + 2\pi\alpha t_2^2\right)} f_T(t_1, t_2) e^{it_1\omega_1 + it_2\omega_2} dt_1 dt_2 \right| \to 0$$

as $\alpha \to 0$.

4. Error analysis

In last section we have proved the convergence property of the regularized Fourier series under the condition $f_T \in L^1(\mathbb{R}^2)$. In this section, we give the error analysis of the regularized Fourier series according to the L^2-norm for the functions $f_T \in L^2(\mathbb{R}^2)$. The bound of the variance of the regularized Fourier series is presented.

By Lemma 3.5, we have next lemma.

Lemma 4.1

$$\sum_{n_1=-\infty}^{\infty} \sum_{n_2=-\infty}^{\infty} \left| \frac{\eta(n_1H_1, n_2H_2)}{[1 + 2\pi\alpha + 2\pi\alpha(n_1H_1)^2][1 + 2\pi\alpha + 2\pi\alpha(n_2H_2)^2]} \right|^2 = O(\delta^2) + O\left(\frac{\delta^2}{\alpha}\right)$$

for $\delta \to +0$ and $\alpha \to +0$, where η and δ are given in Eq. (4) and Eq. (5) in Section 1.

Theorem 4.1 Suppose $f_T \in L^2(\mathbb{R}^2)$ is band-limited. If we choose $\alpha = \alpha(\delta)$ such that $\alpha(\delta) \to 0$ and $\delta^2/\alpha(\delta) \to 0$ as $\delta \to 0$, then $\hat{f}_\alpha(\omega_1, \omega_2) \to \hat{f}_T(\omega_1, \omega_2)$ in $L^2[-\Omega_1, \Omega_1] \times [-\Omega_2, \Omega_2]$ as $\delta \to 0$.

Proof.

$$\hat{f}_\alpha(\omega_1, \omega_2) - \hat{f}_T(\omega_1, \omega_2)$$

$$= H_1H_2 \sum_{n_1=-\infty}^{\infty} \sum_{n_2=-\infty}^{\infty} \frac{[f_T(n_1H_1, n_2H_2) + \eta(n_1H_1, n_2H_2)] e^{in_1H_1\omega_1 + in_2H_2\omega_2}}{\left[1 + 2\pi\alpha + 2\pi\alpha(n_1H_1)^2\right]\left[1 + 2\pi\alpha + 2\pi\alpha(n_2H_2)^2\right]} P_\Omega(\omega_1, \omega_2) - \hat{f}_T(\omega_1, \omega_2)$$

$$= -H_1H_2 \sum_{n_1=-\infty}^{\infty} \sum_{n_2=-\infty}^{\infty} \frac{4\pi\alpha + 2\pi\alpha(n_1H_1)^2 + 2\pi\alpha(n_2H_2)^2 + \left(2\pi\alpha + 2\pi\alpha(n_1H_1)^2\right)\left(2\pi\alpha + 2\pi\alpha(n_2H_2)^2\right)}{\left[1 + 2\pi\alpha + 2\pi\alpha(n_1H_1)^2\right]\left[1 + 2\pi\alpha + 2\pi\alpha(n_2H_2)^2\right]}$$

$$\cdot f_T(n_1H_1, n_2H_2)e^{in_1H_1\omega_1+in_2H_2\omega_2}P_\Omega(\omega_1,\omega_2)$$
$$+H_1H_2\sum_{n_1=-\infty}^{\infty}\sum_{n_2=-\infty}^{\infty}\frac{\eta(n_1H_1,n_2H_2)}{\left[1+2\pi\alpha+2\pi\alpha(n_1H_1)^2\right]\left[1+2\pi\alpha+2\pi\alpha(n_2H_2)^2\right]}$$
$$e^{in_1H_1\omega_1+in_2H_2\omega_2}P_\Omega(\omega_1,\omega_2).$$

Let

$$S(\omega_1,\omega_2):=\sum_{n_1=-\infty}^{\infty}\sum_{n_2=-\infty}^{\infty}$$
$$\frac{4\pi\alpha+2\pi\alpha(n_1H_1)^2+2\pi\alpha(n_2H_2)^2+\left(2\pi\alpha+2\pi\alpha(n_1H_1)^2\right)\left(2\pi\alpha+2\pi\alpha(n_2H_2)^2\right)}{\left[1+2\pi\alpha+2\pi\alpha(n_1H_1)^2\right]\left[1+2\pi\alpha+2\pi\alpha(n_2H_2)^2\right]}$$
$$\cdot f_T(n_1H_1,n_2H_2)e^{in_1H_1\omega_1+in_2H_2\omega_2}P_\Omega(\omega_1,\omega_2).$$

Then

$$\left\|\hat{f}_\alpha(\omega_1,\omega_2)-\hat{f}_T(\omega_1,\omega_2)\right\|_{L^2}^2\le 2H_1^2H_2^2\|S(\omega_1,\omega_2)\|^2+2H_1^2H_2^2$$
$$\left\|\sum_{n_1=-\infty}^{\infty}\sum_{n_2=-\infty}^{\infty}\frac{\eta(n_1H_1,n_2H_2)}{\left[1+2\pi\alpha+2\pi\alpha(n_1H_1)^2\right]\left[1+2\pi\alpha+2\pi\alpha(n_2H_2)^2\right]}e^{in_1H_1\omega_1+in_2H_2\omega_2}P_\Omega(\omega_1,\omega_2)\right\|^2,$$

where

$$\left\|\sum_{n_1=-\infty}^{\infty}\sum_{n_2=-\infty}^{\infty}\frac{\eta(n_1H_1,n_2H_2)}{\left[1+2\pi\alpha+2\pi\alpha(n_1H_1)^2\right]\left[1+2\pi\alpha+2\pi\alpha(n_2H_2)^2\right]}e^{in_1H_1\omega_1+in_2H_2\omega_2}P_\Omega(\omega_1,\omega_2)\right\|^2$$
$$=\sum_{n_1=-\infty}^{\infty}\sum_{n_2=-\infty}^{\infty}\left|\frac{\eta(n_1H_1,n_2H_2)}{\left[1+2\pi\alpha+2\pi\alpha(n_1H_1)^2\right]\left[1+2\pi\alpha+2\pi\alpha(n_2H_2)^2\right]}\right|^2=O\left(\frac{\delta^2}{\alpha}\right)$$

by Lemma 4.1 and

$$\|S(\omega_1,\omega_2)\|^2=\sum_{n_1=-\infty}^{\infty}\sum_{n_2=-\infty}^{\infty}$$
$$\frac{4\pi\alpha+2\pi\alpha(n_1H_1)^2+2\pi\alpha(n_2H_2)^2+\left(2\pi\alpha+2\pi\alpha(n_1H_1)^2\right)\left(2\pi\alpha+2\pi\alpha(n_2H_2)^2\right)}{\left[1+2\pi\alpha+2\pi\alpha(n_1H_1)^2\right]\left[1+2\pi\alpha+2\pi\alpha(n_2H_2)^2\right]}$$
$$\cdot|f_T(n_1H_1,n_2H_2)|^2.$$

For every $\epsilon>0$, there exists $N>0$ such that

$$\sum_{|n_1|\ge N\ or}\sum_{|n_2|\ge N}|f_T(n_1H_1,n_2H_2)|^2<\epsilon,$$

since

$$\sum_{n_1=-\infty}^{\infty}\sum_{n_2=-\infty}^{\infty}$$

$$\frac{4\pi\alpha + 2\pi\alpha(n_1H_1)^2 + 2\pi\alpha(n_2H_2)^2 + \left(2\pi\alpha + 2\pi\alpha(n_1H_1)^2\right)\left(2\pi\alpha + 2\pi\alpha(n_2H_2)^2\right)}{\left[1 + 2\pi\alpha + 2\pi\alpha(n_1H_1)^2\right]\left[1 + 2\pi\alpha + 2\pi\alpha(n_2H_2)^2\right]}$$

$$\cdot\left|f_T(n_1H_1, n_2H_2)\right|^2 = \sum\sum_{|n_1|\le N \text{ and } |n_2|\le N}$$

$$\frac{4\pi\alpha + 2\pi\alpha(n_1H_1)^2 + 2\pi\alpha(n_2H_2)^2 + \left(2\pi\alpha + 2\pi\alpha(n_1H_1)^2\right)\left(2\pi\alpha + 2\pi\alpha(n_2H_2)^2\right)}{\left[1 + 2\pi\alpha + 2\pi\alpha(n_1H_1)^2\right]\left[1 + 2\pi\alpha + 2\pi\alpha(n_2H_2)^2\right]}$$

$$\cdot\left|f_T(n_1H_1, n_2H_2)\right|^2 + \sum\sum_{|n_1|>N \text{ or } |n_2|>N}$$

$$\frac{4\pi\alpha + 2\pi\alpha(n_1H_1)^2 + 2\pi\alpha(n_2H_2)^2 + \left(2\pi\alpha + 2\pi\alpha(n_1H_1)^2\right)\left(2\pi\alpha + 2\pi\alpha(n_2H_2)^2\right)}{\left[1 + 2\pi\alpha + 2\pi\alpha(n_1H_1)^2\right]\left[1 + 2\pi\alpha + 2\pi\alpha(n_2H_2)^2\right]}$$

$$\cdot\left|f_T(n_1H_1, n_2H_2)\right|^2,$$

where

$$\sum\sum_{|n_1|>N \text{ or } |n_2|>N}$$

$$\frac{4\pi\alpha + 2\pi\alpha(n_1H_1)^2 + 2\pi\alpha(n_2H_2)^2 + \left(2\pi\alpha + 2\pi\alpha(n_1H_1)^2\right)\left(2\pi\alpha + 2\pi\alpha(n_2H_2)^2\right)}{\left[1 + 2\pi\alpha + 2\pi\alpha(n_1H_1)^2\right]\left[1 + 2\pi\alpha + 2\pi\alpha(n_2H_2)^2\right]}$$

$$\cdot\left|f_T(n_1H_1, n_2H_2)\right|^2$$

$$\le \sum\sum_{|n_1|\ge N \text{ or } |n_2|\ge N}\left|f_T(n_1H_1, n_2H_2)\right|^2 < \varepsilon$$

and

$$\sum\sum_{|n_1|\le N \text{ and } |n_2|\le N}$$

$$\frac{4\pi\alpha + 2\pi\alpha(n_1H_1)^2 + 2\pi\alpha(n_2H_2)^2 + \left(2\pi\alpha + 2\pi\alpha(n_1H_1)^2\right)\left(2\pi\alpha + 2\pi\alpha(n_2H_2)^2\right)}{\left[1 + 2\pi\alpha + 2\pi\alpha(n_1H_1)^2\right]\left[1 + 2\pi\alpha + 2\pi\alpha(n_2H_2)^2\right]}$$

$$\left|f_T(n_1H_1, n_2H_2)\right|^2 \to 0$$

as $\alpha \to 0$.

Therefore, $\left\|\hat{f}_\alpha(\omega_1, \omega_2) - \hat{f}_T(\omega_1, \omega_2)\right\|_{L^2}^2 \to 0$.

Theorem 4.2 Suppose $f_T \in L^2(\mathbb{R}^2)$ is band-limited. If the noise in Eq. (4) is white noise such that $E[\eta(n_1H_1, n_2H_2)] = 0$ and $Var[\eta(n_1H_1, n_2H_2)] = \sigma^2$, then the bias $\hat{f}_T(\omega_1, \omega_2) - E\left[\hat{f}_\alpha(\omega_1, \omega_2)\right] \to 0$ in $L^2[-\Omega_1, \Omega_1] \times [-\Omega_2, \Omega_2]$ as $\alpha \to 0$ and

$$Var\left[\hat{f}_\alpha(\omega_1, \omega_2)\right] = O(\sigma^2) + O(\sigma^2/\alpha)$$

if $\alpha(\sigma) \to 0$ and $\sigma^2/\alpha(\sigma) \to 0$ as $\sigma \to 0$.

Proof. We can calculate

$$\left\|\hat{f}_T(\omega_1,\omega_2) - E\left[\hat{f}_\alpha(\omega_1,\omega_2)\right]\right\|_{L^2}^2 = H_1^2H_2^2 \cdot \sum_{n_1=-\infty}^{\infty}\sum_{n_2=-\infty}^{\infty}$$

$$\frac{4\pi\alpha + 2\pi\alpha(n_1H_1)^2 + 2\pi\alpha(n_2H_2)^2 + \left(2\pi\alpha + 2\pi\alpha(n_1H_1)^2\right)\left(2\pi\alpha + 2\pi\alpha(n_2H_2)^2\right)}{\left[1 + 2\pi\alpha + 2\pi\alpha(n_1H_1)^2\right]\left[1 + 2\pi\alpha + 2\pi\alpha(n_2H_2)^2\right]}$$

$$\cdot\left|f_T(n_1H_1, n_2H_2)\right|^2$$

and

$$Var\left[\hat{f}_\alpha(\omega_1,\omega_2)\right] = \sum_{n_1=-\infty}^{\infty}\sum_{n_2=-\infty}^{\infty}\frac{\sigma^2}{\left[1 + 2\pi\alpha + 2\pi\alpha(n_1H_1)^2\right]^2\left[1 + 2\pi\alpha + 2\pi\alpha(n_2H_2)^2\right]^2}.$$

By the proof of Theorem 4.1, we can see that $\hat{f}_T(\omega_1,\omega_2) - E\left[\hat{f}_\alpha(\omega_1,\omega_2)\right] \to 0$ in $L^2[-\Omega_1,\Omega_1]\times[-\Omega_2,\Omega_2]$ as $\alpha \to 0$ and $Var\left[\hat{f}_\alpha([-\omega_1,\omega_1])\right] = O(\sigma^2) + O(\sigma^2/\alpha)$.

5. The algorithm and experimental results

In this section, we give the algorithm and an example to show that the regularized Fourier series is more effective in controlling noise than the Fourier series.

In practical computation, we choose a large integer N and use the next formula in computation:

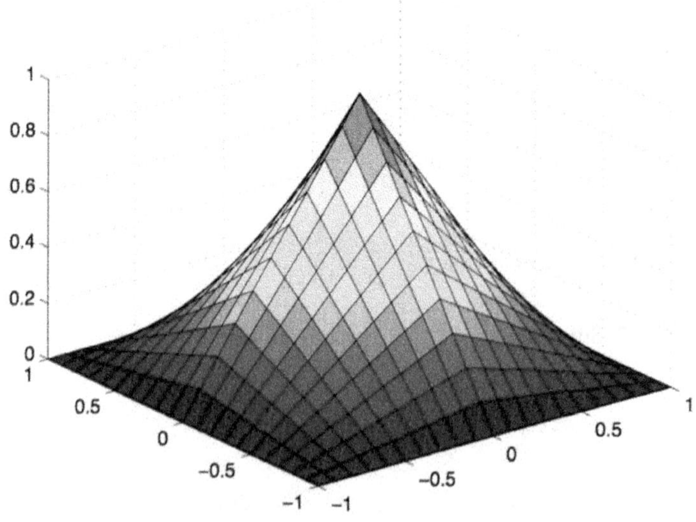

Figure 1.
The exact Fourier transform in Example 2.

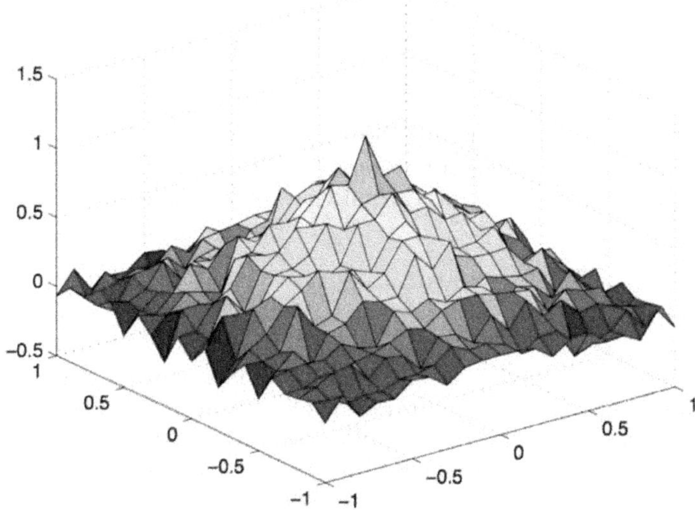

Figure 2.
The numerical results by Fourier series in Example 2.

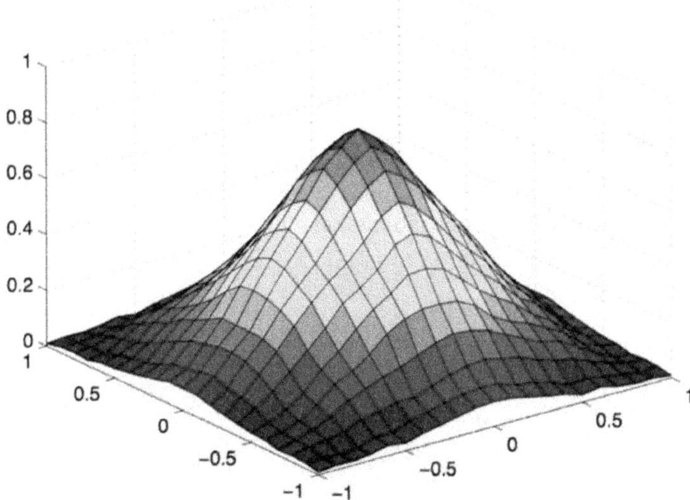

Figure 3.
The numerical results by the regularized Fourier series in Example 2.

$$\hat{f}_{\alpha}(\omega_1,\omega_2) = H_1 H_2 \sum_{n_1=-N}^{N} \sum_{n_2=-N}^{N} \frac{f(n_1 H_1, n_2 H_2) e^{i n_1 H_1 \omega_1 + i n_2 H_2 \omega_2}}{\left[1 + 2\pi\alpha + 2\pi\alpha (n_1 H_1)^2\right]\left[1 + 2\pi\alpha + 2\pi\alpha (n_2 H_2)^2\right]} P_{\Omega}(\omega_1,\omega_2).$$

Example 1. Suppose

$$f_T(t_1,t_2) = \frac{1-\cos t_1}{\pi t_1^2} \frac{1-\cos t_2}{\pi t_2^2}.$$

Then

$$\hat{f}_T(\omega_1, \omega_2) = (1 - |\omega_1|)(1 - |\omega_2|)P_\Omega(\omega_1, \omega_2),$$

where $\Omega_1 = 1$ and $\Omega_2 = 1$.

We add the white noise that is uniformly distributed in $[-0.0005, 0.0005]$ and choose $N = 20$. The exact Fourier transform is in **Figure 1**. The result of the Fourier series is in **Figure 2**. The result of the regularized Fourier series with $\alpha = 0.001$ is in **Figure 3**.

6. Conclusion

The problem of computing the two-dimensional Fourier transform is highly ill-posed. Noise can give rise to large errors if the Fourier series formula is used. The regularized two-dimensional Fourier series is presented. The convergence property is proved and tested by some examples. The convergence property and numerical results show that the regularized two-dimensional Fourier series is excellent in computation in noisy cases. The algorithm will be useful in image processing and multi-dimensional signal processing. The method will be of interest to: engineers who want higher precision in the gauging and design of function generators and analyzers; the electronic or electrical rectification industry; and also to the mathematics community for computing methods and the improvement of mathematics programs on signals and systems, for example, Simulink; and others since many problems in engineering involve noise.

Acknowledgements

The author would like to express appreciation to Sarah Lanand for her help in formatting the document to meet submission guidelines.

Author details

Weidong Chen
Department of Mathematics and Statistics, Minnesota State University, Mankato, United States

*Address all correspondence to: chenw@ksu.edu

References

[1] Soon IY, Koh SN. Speech enhancement using 2-D Fourier transform. IEEE Transactions on Speech and Audio Processing. 2003;**11**(6): 717-724

[2] Li X, Zhang T, Borca CN, Cundiff ST. Many-body interactions in semiconductors probed by optical two-dimensional Fourier transform spectroscopy. Physical Review Letters. 10 February 2006

[3] Siemens ME, Moody G, Li H, Bristow AD, Cundiff ST. Resonance lineshapes in two-dimensional Fourier transform spectroscopy. Optics Express. August 2010;**18**(17)

[4] Goodman JW. Introduction to Fourier Optics. Roberts and Company Publishers; 2005

[5] Kim H, Yang B, Lee B. Iterative Fourier transform algorithm with regularization for the optimal design of diffractive optical elements. Journal of the Optical Society of America A. 2004; **21**(12):2353-2356

[6] Lyuboshenko IV, Akhmetshin AM. Regularization of the problem of image restoration from its noisy Fourier transform phase. In: International Conference on Image Processing, vol. 1. 1996. pp. 793-796

[7] Stein EM, Weiss G. Introduction to Fourier Analysis on Euclidean Spaces (PMS-32). Princeton University Press; 2016

[8] Mahmood F, Toots M, Öfverstedt L, Skoglund U. Algorithm and architecture optimization for 2D discrete Fourier transforms with simultaneous edge artifact removal. International Journal of Reconfigurable Computing. 2018. Article ID 1403181, 17 pages

[9] Shi S, Yang R, You H. A new two-dimensional Fourier transform algorithm based on image sparsity. In: 2017 IEEE International Conference on Acoustics, Speech and Signal Processing (ICASSP); New Orleans, LA. 2017. pp. 1373-1377

[10] Shannon CE. A mathematical theory of communication. The Bell System Technical Journal. July 1948;**27**

[11] Steiner A. Plancherel's theorem and the Shannon series derived simultaneously. The American Mathematical Monthly. Mar. 1980; **87**(3):193-197

[12] Chen W. Computation of Fourier transforms for noisy bandlimited signals. SIAM Journal of Numerical Analysis. 2011;**49**(1):1-14

[13] Chen W. Application of the Regularization Method. LAP LAMBERT Academic Publishing; 2016

[14] Chen W. An efficient method for an ill-posed problem—Band-limited extrapolation by regularization. IEEE Transactions on Signal Processing. 2006;**54**:4611-4618

[15] Tikhonov AN, Arsenin VY. Solution of Ill-Posed Problems. Winston/Wiley; 1977

Section 5

Applications in the Integral Forms Discurse of Mathematical Physics Equations

Chapter 5

Electro-magnetic Simulation Based on the Integral Form of Maxwell's Equations

Naofumi Kitsunezaki

Abstract

Algorithms for a computational method of electromagnetics based on the integral form of Maxwell's equations are introduced. The algorithms are supported by the lowest- and next-to-the-lowest-order approximations of integrals over a cell surface and edge of the equations. The method supported by the lowest-order approximation of the integrals coincides with the original finite-difference time-domain (FDTD) method, a well-known computational method of electromagnetics based on the differential form of Maxwell's equations. The method supported by the next-to-the-lowest-order approximation can be considered a correction to the FDTD method. Numerical results of an electromagnetic wave propagating in a two-dimensional slab waveguide using the original and the corrected FDTD methods are also shown to compare them with an analytical result. In addition, the results of the corrected FDTD method are also shown to be more accurate and reliable than those of the original FDTD method.

Keywords: Maxwell's equations, integral form, finite-difference time-domain method, the lowest-order approximation, next-to-the-lowest-order approximation, computational method

1. Introduction

Maxwell's equations are considered the fundamental equations of an electromagnetic field. They consist of laws of Faraday, Ampére-Maxwell, and Gauss for magnetic and electric flux densities

$$\partial_t \boldsymbol{B} = -\nabla \times \boldsymbol{E}, \tag{1}$$

$$\partial_t \boldsymbol{D} = \nabla \times \boldsymbol{H} - \boldsymbol{i}, \tag{2}$$

$$\nabla \cdot \boldsymbol{B} = 0, \tag{3}$$

$$\nabla \cdot \boldsymbol{D} = \rho, \tag{4}$$

where $\boldsymbol{E}$ and $\boldsymbol{H}$ are electric and magnetic fields, respectively, $\boldsymbol{D}$ and $\boldsymbol{B}$ are electric and magnetic flux densities, respectively, $\boldsymbol{i}$ is current density, ρ is charge density, $\partial_t f$ is the time derivative of field$f$, $\nabla \times \boldsymbol{A}$ is the rotation of vector field $\boldsymbol{A}$, $\nabla \cdot \boldsymbol{A}$ is the divergence of vector $\boldsymbol{A}$, and ρ is the electric charge density. Taking the divergence of both sides of Eq. (2) and using Eq. (4), law of charge conservation is derived:

$$\partial_t \rho + \nabla \cdot \boldsymbol{i} = 0. \tag{5}$$

Maxwell's equations combined with law of Lorentz are the foundation of electronics, optics, and electric circuits used to understand the physical structure dependence of an electromagnetic field distribution, the interaction between the structure and field, and other relevant characteristics. However, situations having analytical solutions of them are rare. Thus, computational method of electromagnetics is important.

For computational methods of electromagnetics, there are two major types, time domain and frequency domain. In a time-domain method, time is discretized. The field distribution of a particular time step is determined by Maxwell's equations and by the distribution of the previous time step. In a frequency-domain method, the time derivative is replaced by $i\omega$, where i is the imaginary unit and ω is the angular frequency. Thus, Maxwell's equations are solved. A user chooses a method by considering the analysis object, calculation accuracy, specifications of his or her computer, and other relevant factors.

The finite-difference time-domain (FDTD) method is a time-domain method used to analyze high-frequency electromagnetic phenomena in optical devices, antennae, and similar devices [1]. Its algorithm is based on the laws of Faraday (1), Ampére-Maxwell (2), and charge conservation (5). In the FDTD method, Gauss's laws (3) and (4) are not considered except for the initial condition. The reason can be easily understood by taking divergence of both sides of Eq. (1) and (2), and combining the charge conservation law (5) yields

$$\partial_t \nabla \cdot \boldsymbol{B} = 0, \tag{6}$$

$$\partial_t (\nabla \cdot \boldsymbol{D} - \rho) = 0, \tag{7}$$

the time derivatives of Eq. (3) and (4), respectively. This means that Gauss's laws of electric and magnetic flux densities are always satisfied when they are initially satisfied.

In the next section, an algorithm of the original FDTD method is shown. Next, a corrected algorithm of the FDTD method based on the integral form of Maxwell's equations is shown [2, 3]. Then, a numerical result of the propagation of electromagnetic waves in a two-dimensional slab waveguide is shown. In the subsequent section, the accuracy of the original and corrected FDTD methods is compared by showing the differences between the computational and analytical methods. The analytical method is shown in the appendix. The last section is devoted to conclusions.

2. Algorithm of the FDTD Method

The FDTD method is a computational method for analyzing the space-time dependence of electromagnetic fields by discretizing space-time variables. This method utilizes a dual lattice called a Yee lattice [1].

Figure 1 shows the Yee lattice. In the figure, there are two cubes called cells. The component parallel to the edge of the electric field is at the center of each edge of a yellow cell. The component perpendicular to the surface of the magnetic field is at the center of each surface of the cell. The cyan cell is placed in such a manner that the component parallel to the edge of the magnetic field is at the center

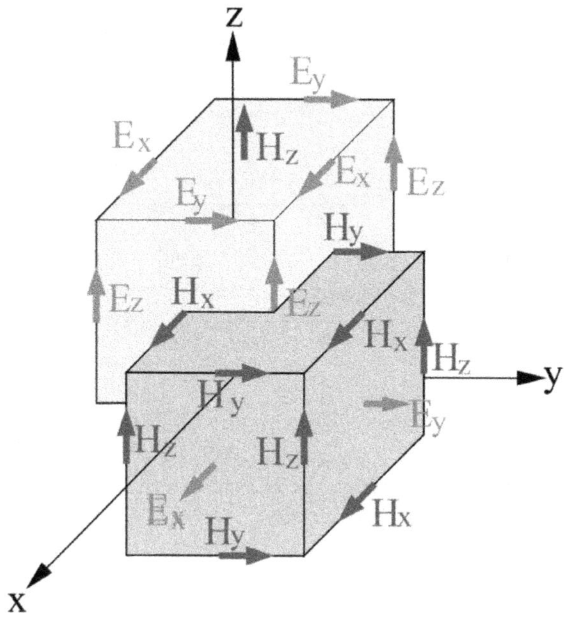

Figure 1.
Yee lattice used in the FDTD method.

of its edge, and the component normal to the surface of the electric field is at the center of its surface.

The yellow cell is used to calculate the magnetic field at time $t = t_0 + \Delta t$ using the magnetic field at $t = t_0$ and the electric field at $t = t_0 + \frac{1}{2}\Delta t$ by applying Eq. (1), where t_0 is a particular time and Δt is the time step. Let us now consider the top surface of the cell. At the center of the surface whose coordinates are (x_0, y_0, z_0), Eq. (1) becomes

$$\partial_t B_z(t, x_0, y_0, z_0) = -\partial_x E_y(t, x_0, y_0, z_0) + \partial_y E_x(t, x_0, y_0, z_0), \tag{8}$$

where the variables x, y, and z of B and E represent the x-, y-, and z-components of the B and E fields, respectively, and ∂_x and ∂_y represent the partial derivatives in the x- and y-directions, respectively. Replacing the partial derivatives by the central differences yields

$$\partial_t B_z(t, x_0, y_0, z_0) = \frac{B_z(t_0 + \Delta t, x_0, y_0, z_0) - B_z(t_0, x_0, y_0, z_0)}{\Delta t} + O(\Delta t)^2, \tag{9}$$

$$\partial_x E_y(t, x_0, y_0, z_0) = \frac{E_y\left(t_0 + \frac{1}{2}\Delta t, x_0 + \frac{1}{2}\Delta x, y_0, z_0\right) - E_y\left(t_0 + \frac{1}{2}\Delta t, x_0 - \frac{1}{2}\Delta x, y_0, z_0\right)}{\Delta x} + O(\Delta y)^2, \tag{10}$$

$$\partial_y E_x(t, x_0, y_0, z_0) = \frac{E_x\left(t_0 + \frac{1}{2}\Delta t, x_0, y_0 + \frac{1}{2}\Delta y, z_0\right) - E_x\left(t_0 + \frac{1}{2}\Delta t, x_0, y_0 - \frac{1}{2}\Delta y, z_0\right)}{\Delta y} + O(\Delta x)^2, \tag{11}$$

where $t = t_0 + \frac{1}{2}\Delta t$. Then, $B_z(t_0 + \Delta t, x_0, y_0, z_0)$ are derived from Eqs. (9), (10), and (11) as the following:

$$B_z(t_0+\Delta t,x_0,y_0,z_0)=B_z(t_0,x_0,y_0,z_0)+\Delta t\left[-\frac{E_y\left(t_0+\frac{1}{2}\Delta t,x_0+\frac{1}{2}\Delta x,y_0,z_0\right)}{\Delta x}\right.$$

$$+\frac{E_y\left(t_0+\frac{1}{2}\Delta t,x_0-\frac{1}{2}\Delta x,y_0,z_0\right)}{\Delta x}+\frac{E_x\left(t_0+\frac{1}{2}\Delta t,x_0,y_0+\frac{1}{2}\Delta y,z_0\right)}{\Delta y}$$

$$\left.-\frac{E_x\left(t_0+\frac{1}{2}\Delta t,x_0,y_0-\frac{1}{2}\Delta y,z_0\right)}{\Delta y}+O(\Delta x,\Delta y)^2\right]+O(\Delta t)^3. \tag{12}$$

where $O(\Delta x, \Delta y)^2$ means $\sum_{m+n\geq 2, m,n\geq 2}O((\Delta x)^m(\Delta y)^n)$. B_x and B_y at $t=t_0+\Delta t$ can also be derived similarly. Usually, the $\boldsymbol{H}$ field can be derived from the $\boldsymbol{B}$ field. For example, in vacuum, air, or a dielectric

$$\boldsymbol{H}=\frac{1}{\mu_0}\boldsymbol{B}, \tag{13}$$

where μ_0 is the vacuum permeability with the value $4\pi\times 10^{-7}\ [Vs/Am]$. In a magnetic material, the relationship between $\boldsymbol{H}$ and $\boldsymbol{B}$ often becomes nontrivial, but this is beyond the scope of this book. However, in small $\boldsymbol{H}$ and $\boldsymbol{B}$ regions, it can be approximated by the following equation:

$$\boldsymbol{H}=\frac{1}{\mu}\boldsymbol{B}, \tag{14}$$

where μ depends on the material. Often, a value

$$\mu^*=\frac{\mu}{\mu_0}, \tag{15}$$

called the relative permeability is used. In an optical wavelength region, μ_0 is 1.

The cyan cell is used to calculate the electric field at $t=t_0+\frac{1}{2}\Delta t$ using the electric field at $t=t_0-\frac{1}{2}\Delta t$ and the magnetic field at $t=t-\Delta t$ applying Eq. (2) representing Ampére-Maxwell's law. Let us consider the right-hand surface of the cell. At the center of the surface whose coordinates are (x_1,y_1,z_1), Eq. (2) becomes

$$\partial_t D_y(t,x_1,y_1,z_1)=\partial_z H_x(t,x_1,y_1,z_1)-\partial_x H_z(t,x_1,y_1,z_1)-i_y(t,x_1,y_1,z_1). \tag{16}$$

Replacing partial derivatives with central differences yields

$$\partial_t D_y(t,x_1,y_1,z_1)=\frac{D_y(t_0+\Delta t,x_1,y_1,z_1)-D_y(t_0,x_1,y_1,z_1)}{\Delta t}+O(\Delta t)^2, \tag{17}$$

$$\partial_x H_z(t,x_1,y_1,z_1)=\frac{H_z(t_0+\frac{1}{2}\Delta t,x_1+\frac{1}{2}\Delta x,y_1,z_1)-H_z(t_0+\frac{1}{2}\Delta t,x_1-\frac{1}{2}\Delta x,y_1,z_1)}{\Delta x}+O(\Delta x)^2, \tag{18}$$

$$\partial_z H_x(t, x_1, y_1, z_1) = \frac{H_x\left(t_0 + \frac{1}{2}\Delta t, x_1, y_1, z_1 + \frac{1}{2}\Delta z\right) - H_x\left(t_0 + \frac{1}{2}\Delta t, x_1, y_1, z_1 - \frac{1}{2}\Delta z\right)}{\Delta z} + O(\Delta z)^2, \tag{19}$$

where $t = t_0$. Then, $D_y(t_0, x_1, y_1, z_1)$ is derived as follows:

$$D_y\left(t_0 + \frac{1}{2}\Delta t, x_1, y_1, z_1\right) = D_y\left(t_0 - \frac{1}{2}, x_1, y_1, z_1\right) + \Delta t \left[\frac{H_x\left(t_0, x_1, y_1, z_1 + \frac{1}{2}\Delta z\right)}{\Delta z}\right.$$

$$- \frac{H_x\left(t_0, x_1, y_1, z_1 - \frac{1}{2}\Delta z\right)}{\Delta z} - \frac{H_z\left(t_0, x_1 + \frac{1}{2}\Delta x, y_1, z_1\right)}{\Delta x} + \frac{H_z\left(t_0, x_1 - \frac{1}{2}\Delta x, y_1, z_1\right)}{\Delta x}$$

$$\left. -i_y(t_0, x_1, y_1, z_1) + O(\Delta x, \Delta z)^2 \right] + O(\Delta t)^3. \tag{20}$$

D_x and D_z at $t = t_0 + \Delta t$ can also be derived similarly. Typically, the $\boldsymbol{E}$ field can be derived from the $\boldsymbol{D}$ flux density. For example, in vacuum, air, or magnetic material

$$\boldsymbol{E} = \frac{1}{\varepsilon_0}\boldsymbol{D}, \tag{21}$$

where ε_0 is the vacuum permittivity, whose value is $8.85418782 \times 10^{-12}$ $[As/Vm]$. In a dielectric material, the relationship between **E** and **D** often becomes nontrivial, but this is beyond the scope of this book. However, in small **E** and **D** regions, it can be approximated by

$$\boldsymbol{E} = \frac{1}{\varepsilon}\boldsymbol{D}, \tag{22}$$

where ε depends on the material. Often a value

$$\varepsilon^* = \frac{\varepsilon}{\varepsilon_0}, \tag{23}$$

called the relative permittivity and a value

$$n = \sqrt{\varepsilon^*}, \tag{24}$$

called the index, is used.

Figure 2 shows the algorithm of the FDTD method for the case in which Eqs. (14) and (22) are satisfied. Initially, distributions of the $\boldsymbol{E}$ and $\boldsymbol{H}$ fields are given which in turn satisfy Eqs. (3) and (4). When the $\boldsymbol{E}$ field distribution at $t = t_0 - \Delta t/2$ and the $\boldsymbol{H}$ field distribution at $t = t_0$ are known, the $\boldsymbol{E}$ field at $t = t_0 + \Delta t/2$ is calculated using Eqs. (20) and (22), given the $\boldsymbol{E}$ field at $t = t_0 - \Delta t/2$ and the $\boldsymbol{H}$ field at $t = t_0$. The $\boldsymbol{H}$ field at $t = t_0 + \Delta t$ is calculated using Eqs. (12) and (14), given the $\boldsymbol{H}$ field at $t = t_0$, having determined the $\boldsymbol{E}$ field at $t = t_0 + \Delta t/2$. If the time t is less than t_{fin}, then the time becomes $t + \Delta t$ and the flow repeats. If the time t exceeds t_{fin}, the algorithm terminates.

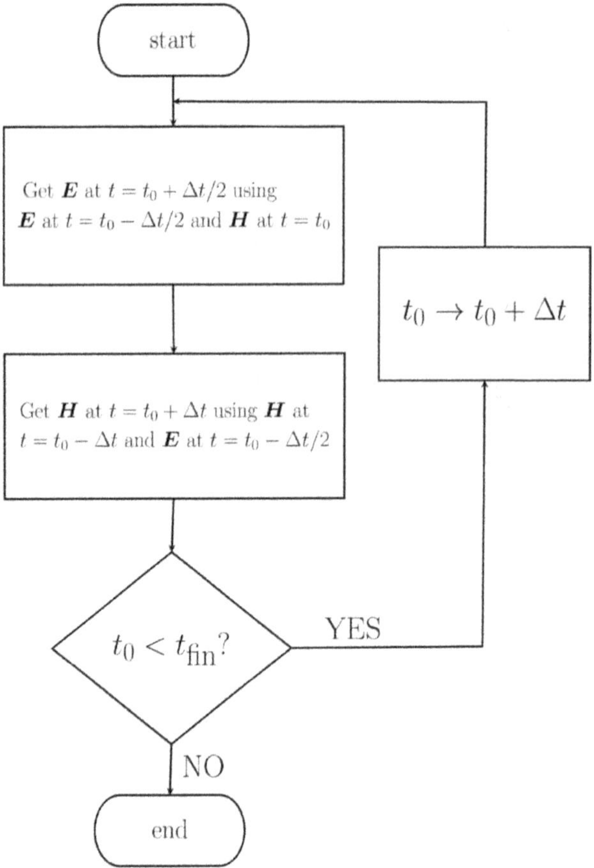

Figure 2.
Flow of the FDTD algorithm.

3. Integral form of Maxwell's equation and a correction to the FDTD method

The FDTD method is a numerical method for solving Maxwell's equations using a computer. Any computer can have a finite number of degrees of freedom because it has a finite memory size. In contrast, an electromagnetic field in continuum space has infinitely many degrees of freedom, because the field exists at every point of the space–time continuum. Therefore, Maxwell's equations must be suitably approximated for us to be able to calculate them using a computer. The algorithm shown in the previous section appears to be suitable for this purpose, because only finitely many degrees of freedom are used to calculate an electromagnetic field distribution if the calculation area is compact.

Note that Eqs. (12) and (20) are exact on a Yee lattice only after taking a zero cell size limit. This appears to cause no problem, but, there is an example in elementary particle physics showing that the discretized continuum theory is different from the original continuum theory [4]. In this example, a fermion in discretized quantum field theory generates nonphysical fermionic degrees of freedom. This problem is called fermion doubling. In essence, this phenomenon is caused by replacing differentials with differences as in Eqs. (9)–(10) and (17)–(19).

An algorithm in which differentials are not replaced with differences must be considered in order to avoid such problems.

As a result of Stokes' theorem, Faraday's and Ampére-Maxwell's laws in Eqs. (1) and (2) can be written in an integral form as

$$\frac{d}{dt}\int_S d\boldsymbol{a}\cdot\mathbf{B} = -\int_{\partial S} d\boldsymbol{s}\cdot\mathbf{E}, \tag{25}$$

$$\frac{d}{dt}\int_S d\boldsymbol{a}\cdot\mathbf{D} = \int_{\partial S} d\boldsymbol{s}\cdot\boldsymbol{H} - \int_S d\boldsymbol{a}\cdot\boldsymbol{i}, \tag{26}$$

where S is a compact and connected surface, ∂S is the boundary curve of the surface, $d\boldsymbol{a}$ is a surface element normal to the surface, and $d\boldsymbol{s}$ is a line element parallel to the curve. Moreover, integrating both sides of Eq. (25) over t from $t = t_0$ to $t_0 + \Delta t$ and those of Eq. (26) over t from $t = t_0 - \Delta t/2$ to $t_0 + \Delta t/2$ yields

$$\int_S d\boldsymbol{a}\cdot\mathbf{B}(t_0+\Delta t,x,y,z) = \int_S d\boldsymbol{a}\cdot\mathbf{B}(t_0,x,y,z) - \int_{t_0}^{t_0+\Delta t} dt\int_{\partial S} d\boldsymbol{s}\cdot\mathbf{E}(t,x,y,z), \tag{27}$$

$$\begin{aligned}\int_S d\mathbf{a}\cdot\mathbf{D}(t_0+\Delta t/2,x,y,z) &= \int_S d\boldsymbol{a}\cdot\mathbf{D}(t_0-\Delta t/2,x,y,z)\\ &+\int_{t_0-\Delta t/2}^{t_0+\Delta t/2} dt\left[\int_{\partial S} d\boldsymbol{s}\cdot\mathbf{H}(t,x,y,z) - \int_S d\boldsymbol{a}\cdot\boldsymbol{i}(t,x,y,z)\right].\end{aligned} \tag{28}$$

Note that no derivative is used in Eqs. (27) and (28), with the result that problems such as fermion doubling cannot occur. Our problem is how to approximate the integrals in Eqs. (27) and (28).

In general, when f is analytical in a region including $\xi_0 - \Delta\xi/2 \le \xi \le \xi_0 + \Delta\xi/2$, the following relationship is satisfied:

$$\int_{\xi_0-\Delta\xi/2}^{\xi_0+\Delta\xi/2} d\xi f(\xi) = \int_{\xi_0-\Delta\xi/2}^{\xi_0+\Delta\xi/2} d\xi \sum_{n=0}^{\infty}\frac{1}{n!}\frac{d^n f(\xi_0)}{d\xi^n}(\xi-\xi_0)^n, \tag{29}$$

and when g is analytical in a region including $\xi_0 - \Delta\xi/2 \le \xi \le \xi_0 + \Delta\xi/2$ and $\eta_0 - \Delta\eta/2 \le \eta \le \eta_0 + \Delta\eta/2$, the following relationship is satisfied:

$$\int_{\xi_0-\Delta\xi/2}^{\xi_0+\Delta\xi/2} d\xi \int_{\eta_0-\Delta\eta/2}^{\eta_0+\Delta\eta/2} d\eta g(\xi,\eta) = \int_{\xi_0-\Delta\xi/2}^{\xi_0+\Delta\xi/2} d\xi \int_{\eta_0-\Delta\eta/2}^{\eta_0+\Delta\eta/2} d\eta \sum_{m,\,n=0}^{\infty}\frac{1}{m!n!}\frac{\partial^{m+n}g(\xi_0,\eta_0)}{\partial\xi^m\partial\eta^n}(\xi-\xi_0)^m(\eta-\eta_0)^n. \tag{30}$$

The lowest-order approximations of Eqs. (29) and (30) are, respectively,

$$\int_{\xi_0-\Delta\xi/2}^{\xi_0+\Delta\xi/2} d\xi f(\xi) = f(\xi_0)\Delta\xi + O(\Delta\xi)^3, \tag{31}$$

$$\int_{\xi_0-\Delta\xi/2}^{\xi_0+\Delta\xi/2} d\xi \int_{\eta_0-\Delta\eta/2}^{\eta_0+\Delta\eta/2} d\eta g(\xi,\eta) = g(\xi_0,\eta_0)\Delta\xi\Delta\eta + O\left((\Delta\xi,\Delta\eta)^4\right). \tag{32}$$

An algorithm for the FDTD method supported by the lowest-order approximation of the integral form of Maxwell's equations is derived by applying Eqs. (31) and (32) to Eqs. (27) and (28). When S is the top surface of the yellow cell in **Figure 1**, Eq. (27) is approximated as

$$\begin{aligned} B_z(t_0+\Delta t, x_0, y_0, z_0)\Delta x\Delta y = B_z(t_0, x_0, y_0, z_0)\Delta x\Delta y - \big[E_y(t+\Delta t/2, x_0+\Delta x/2, y_0, z_0)\Delta y \\ - E_x(t+\Delta t/2, x_0, y_0+\Delta y/2, z_0)\Delta x - E_y(t+\Delta t/2, x_0-\Delta x/2, y_0, z_0)\Delta y \\ + E_x(t+\Delta t/2, x_0, y_0-\Delta y/2, z_0)\Delta x\big]\Delta t + O(\Delta t)^3, \end{aligned} \tag{33}$$

where (x_0, y_0, z_0) is the center coordinates of the surface. Comparison of Eq. (12) with Eq. (33) reveals that they are essentially the same.

When S is the right surface of the cyan cell in **Figure 1**, Eq. (28) can be approximated as

$$\begin{aligned} D_y(t_0+\Delta t/2, x_1, y_1, z_1)\Delta x\Delta z = D_y(t_0-\Delta t/2, x_1, y_1, z_1)\Delta x\Delta z + \big[H_x(t_0, x_1, y_1, z_1+\Delta z/2)\Delta x \\ - H_z(t_0, x_1+\Delta x/2, y_1, z_1)\Delta z - H_x(t_0, x_1, y_1, z_1-\Delta z/2)\Delta x + H_z(t_0, x_1-\Delta x/2, y_1, z_1)\Delta z \\ - i_y(t_0, x_1, y_1, z_1)\Delta x\Delta z\big]\Delta t + O(\Delta t)^3, \end{aligned} \tag{34}$$

where (x_1, y_1, z_1) is the center coordinates of the surface. Comparison of Eq. (20) with Eq. (34) reveals that they are essentially the same. Therefore, the original FDTD method, which is based on the differential form of Maxwell's equations, is the same as the FDTD method supported by the lowest-order approximation of the integral form of those equations.

Next, an algorithm for the FDTD method supported by the next-to-the-lowest-order approximation of the integral form of Maxwell's equation is derived. In this case, the next-to-the-lowest-order approximation is applied only in the spatial directions, and the lowest-order approximation is applied in the time direction. Hereafter, the FDTD method supported by the next-to-the-lowest-order approximation of integrals is called the corrected FDTD method.

In general, the next-to-the-lowest-order approximations of Eqs. (29) and (30) are, respectively,

$$\int_{\xi_0-\Delta\xi/2}^{\xi_0+\Delta\xi/2} d\xi f(\xi) = f(\xi_0)\Delta\xi + \frac{1}{24}\frac{d^2 f(\xi_0)}{d\xi^2}(\Delta\xi)^3 + O(\Delta\xi)^5, \tag{35}$$

$$\begin{aligned} \int_{\xi_0-\Delta\xi/2}^{\xi_0+\Delta\xi/2} d\xi \int_{\eta_0-\Delta\eta/2}^{\eta_0+\Delta\eta/2} d\eta g(\xi,\eta) = g(\xi_0,\eta_0)\Delta\xi\Delta\eta + \frac{1}{24}\left(\frac{\partial^2 g(\xi,\eta)}{\partial\xi^2}(\Delta\xi)^3\Delta\eta + \frac{\partial^2 g(\xi,\eta)}{\partial\eta^2}\Delta\xi(\Delta\eta)^3\right) \\ + O(\Delta\xi,\Delta\eta)^6. \end{aligned} \tag{36}$$

When S is the top surface of the yellow cell in **Figure 1**, Eq. (27) is approximated by applying Eqs. (35) and (36) to yield

$$
\begin{aligned}
&B_z(t_0+\Delta t,x_0,y_0,z_0)\Delta x\Delta y+\frac{1}{24}\left[\partial_x^2 B_z(t_0+\Delta t,x_0,y_0,z_0)(\Delta x)^3\Delta y\right.\\
&\quad\left.+\partial_y^2 B_z(t_0+\Delta t,x_0,y_0,z_0)\Delta x(\Delta y)^3\right]\\
&=B_z(t_0,x_0,y_0,z_0)\Delta x\Delta y+\frac{1}{24}\left[\partial_x^2 B_z(t_0,x_0,y_0,z_0)(\Delta x)^3\Delta y+\partial_y^2 B_z(t_0,x_0,y_0,z_0)\Delta x(\Delta y)^3\right]\\
&-\left[E_y(t+\Delta t/2,x_0+\Delta x/2,y_0,z_0)\Delta y+\frac{1}{24}\partial_y^2 E_y(t+\Delta t/2,x_0+\Delta x/2,y_0,z_0)(\Delta y)^3\right.\\
&-E_x(t+\Delta t/2,x_0,y_0+\Delta y/2,z_0)\Delta x-\frac{1}{24}\partial_x^2 E_x(t+\Delta t/2,x_0,y_0+\Delta y/2,z_0)(\Delta x)^3\\
&-E_y(t+\Delta t/2,x_0-\Delta x/2,y_0,z_0)\Delta y-\frac{1}{24}\partial_y^2 E_y(t+\Delta t/2,x_0-\Delta x/2,y_0,z_0)(\Delta y)^3\\
&\left.+E_x(t+\Delta t/2,x_0,y_0-\Delta y/2,z_0)\Delta x+\frac{1}{24}\partial_x^2 E_x(t+\Delta t/2,x_0,y_0-\Delta y/2,z_0)(\Delta x)^3\right]\Delta t+O(\Delta t)^3.
\end{aligned}
\tag{37}
$$

When S is the right-hand surface of the cyan cell in **Figure 1**, Eq. (28) is approximated by applying Eqs. (35) and (36) to yield

$$
\begin{aligned}
&D_y(t_0+\Delta t/2,x_1,y_1,z_1)\Delta x\Delta z+\frac{1}{24}\left[\partial_x^2 D_y(t_0+\Delta t/2,x_1,y_1,z_1)(\Delta x)^3\Delta y\right.\\
&\quad\left.+\partial_y^2 D_y(t_0+\Delta t/2,x_1,y_1,z_1)\Delta x(\Delta y)^3\right]\\
&=D_y(t_0-\Delta t/2,x_1,y_1,z_1)\Delta x\Delta z+\frac{1}{24}\left[\partial_x^2 D_y(t_0-\Delta t/2,x_1,y_1,z_1)(\Delta x)^3\Delta y\right.\\
&\quad\left.+\partial_y^2 D_y(t_0-\Delta t/2,x_1,y_1,z_1)\Delta x(\Delta y)^3\right]\\
&\quad+\left[H_x(t_0,x_1,y_1,z_1+\Delta z/2)\Delta x+\frac{1}{24}\partial_x^2 H_x(t_0,x_1,y_1,z_1+\Delta z/2)(\Delta x)^3\right.\\
&\quad-H_z(t_0,x_1+\Delta x/2,y_1,z_1)\Delta z-\frac{1}{24}\partial_z^2 H_z(t_0,x_1+\Delta x/2,y_1,z_1)(\Delta z)^3\\
&\quad-H_x(t_0,x_1,y_1,z_1-\Delta z/2)\Delta x-\frac{1}{24}\partial_x^2 H_x(t_0,x_1,y_1,z_1-\Delta z/2)(\Delta x)^3\\
&\quad+H_z(t_0,x_1-\Delta x/2,y_1,z_1)\Delta z+\frac{1}{24}\partial_z^2 H_z(t_0,x_1-\Delta x/2,y_1,z_1)(\Delta z)^3\\
&\quad-i_y(t_0,x_1,y_1,z_1)\Delta x\Delta z-\frac{1}{24}\partial_x^2 i_y(t_0,x_1,y_1,z_1)(\Delta x)^2\Delta z\\
&\quad\left.-\frac{1}{24}\partial_z^2 i_y(t_0,x_1,y_1,z_1)\Delta x(\Delta z)^2\right]\Delta t+O(\Delta t)^3.
\end{aligned}
\tag{38}
$$

There are second derivatives in Eqs. (37) and (38), but they are not calculated in the FDTD method. Therefore, the second derivatives are determined from the calculated electromagnetic field. To determine the second derivatives, the relationship

$$f(\xi_0 + \Delta\xi) + f(\xi_0 - \Delta\xi) = 2f(\xi) + \frac{d^2 f(\xi_0)}{d\xi^2}(\Delta\xi)^2 + O(\Delta\xi)^4, \tag{39}$$

for any function f is applied. Applying Eq. (39) to Eq. (37) yields

$$\begin{aligned}
&\left[\frac{5}{6}B_z(t_0+\Delta t, x_0, y_0, z_0) + \frac{1}{24}(B_z(t_0+\Delta t, x_0+\Delta x, y_0, z_0) + B_z(t_0+\Delta t, x_0-\Delta x, y_0, z_0)\right.\\
&\quad\left. + B_z(t_0+\Delta t, x_0, y_0+\Delta y, z_0) + B_z(t_0+\Delta t, x_0, y_0-\Delta y, z_0))\right] x\Delta y\\
&= \left[\frac{5}{6}B_z(t_0, x_0, y_0, z_0) + \frac{1}{24}(B_z(t_0, x_0+\Delta x, y_0, z_0) + B_z(t_0, x_0-\Delta x, y_0, z_0)\right.\\
&\quad\left. + B_z(t_0, x_0, y_0+\Delta y, z_0) + B_z(t_0, x_0, y_0-\Delta y, z_0))\right]\Delta x\Delta y\\
&\quad - \left\{\left[\frac{11}{12}E_y(t+\Delta t/2, x_0+\Delta x/2, y_0, z_0) + \frac{1}{24}(E_y(t+\Delta t/2, x_0+\Delta x/2, y_0+\Delta y, z_0)\right.\right.\\
&\quad\left. + E_y(t+\Delta t/2, x_0+\Delta x/2, y_0-\Delta y, z_0))\right]\Delta y - \left[\frac{11}{12}E_x(t+\Delta t/2, x_0, y_0+\Delta y/2, z_0)\right.\\
&\quad\left. + \frac{1}{24}(E_x(t+\Delta t/2, x_0+\Delta x, y_0+\Delta y/2, z_0) + E_x(t+\Delta t/2, x_0-\Delta x, y_0+\Delta y/2, z_0))\right]\Delta x\\
&\quad - \left[\frac{11}{12}E_y(t+\Delta t/2, x_0-\Delta x/2, y_0, z_0) + \frac{1}{24}(E_y(t+\Delta t/2, x_0-\Delta x/2, y_0+\Delta y, z_0)\right.\\
&\quad\left. + E_y(t+\Delta t/2, x_0-\Delta x/2, y_0-\Delta y, z_0))\right]\Delta y + \left[\frac{11}{12}E_x(t+\Delta t/2, x_0, y_0-\Delta y/2, z_0)\right.\\
&\quad\left.\left. + \frac{1}{24}(E_x(t+\Delta t/2, x_0+\Delta x, y_0-\Delta y/2, z_0) + E_x(t+\Delta t/2, x_0-\Delta x, y_0-\Delta y/2, z_0))\right]\Delta x\right\}\Delta t\\
&\quad + O(\Delta t)^3.
\end{aligned} \tag{40}$$

Applying Eq. (39) to Eq. (38) yields

$$\begin{aligned}
&\left[\frac{5}{6}D_y(t_0+\Delta t/2, x_1, y_1, z_1) + \frac{1}{24}(D_y(t_0+\Delta t/2, x_1+\Delta x, y_1, z_1) + D_y(t_0+\Delta t/2, x_1-\Delta x, y_1, z_1)\right.\\
&\quad\left. + D_y(t_0+\Delta t/2, x_1, y_1, z_1+\Delta z) + D_y(t_0+\Delta t/2, x_1, y_1, z_1-\Delta z))\right]\Delta x\Delta z\\
&= \left[\frac{5}{6}D_y(t_0-\Delta t/2, x_1, y_1, z_1) + \frac{1}{24}(D_y(t_0-\Delta t/2, x_1+\Delta x, y_1, z_1) + D_y(t_0-\Delta t/2, x_1-\Delta x, y_1, z_1)\right.\\
&\quad\left. + D_y(t_0-\Delta t/2, x_1, y_1, z_1+\Delta z) + D_y(t_0-\Delta t/2, x_1, y_1, z_1-\Delta z))\right]\Delta x\Delta z\\
&\quad + \left\{\left[\frac{11}{12}H_x(t_0, x_1, y_1, z_1+\Delta z/2) + \frac{1}{24}(H_x(t_0, x_1+\Delta x, y_1, z_1+\Delta z/2) + H_x(t_0, x_1-\Delta x, y_1, z_1+\Delta z/2))\right]\Delta x\right.\\
&\quad - \left[\frac{11}{12}H_z(t_0, x_1+\Delta x/2, y_1, z_1) + \frac{1}{24}(H_z(t_0, x_1+\Delta x/2, y_1, z_1+\Delta z) + H_z(t_0, x_1+\Delta x/2, y_1, z_1-\Delta z))\right]\Delta z\\
&\quad - \left[\frac{11}{12}H_x(t_0, x_1, y_1, z_1-\Delta z/2) + \frac{1}{24}(H_x(t_0, x_1+\Delta x, y_1, z_1-\Delta z/2) + H_x(t_0, x_1-\Delta x, y_1, z_1-\Delta z/2))\right]\Delta x\\
&\quad + \left[\frac{11}{12}H_z(t_0, x_1-\Delta x/2, y_1, z_1) + \frac{1}{24}(H_z(t_0, x_1-\Delta x/2, y_1, z_1+\Delta z) + H_z(t_0, x_1-\Delta x/2, y_1, z_1-\Delta z))\right]\Delta z\\
&\quad - \left[\frac{5}{6}i_y(t_0, x_1, y_1, z_1) + \frac{1}{24}(i_y(t_0, x_1+\Delta x, y_1, z_1) + i_y(t_0, x_1-\Delta x, y_1, z_1) + i_y(t_0, x_1, y_1, z_1+\Delta z)\right.\\
&\quad\left.\left. + i_y(t_0, x_1, y_1, z_1-\Delta z))\right]\Delta x\Delta z\right\}\Delta t + O(\Delta t)^3.
\end{aligned} \tag{41}$$

Note that points $(x_i \pm \Delta x, y_i, z_i)$ and $(x_i, y_i, z_i \pm \Delta z)$ are at adjacent cells to the cell including (x_i, y_i, z_i). Therefore, all terms in Eqs. (40) and (41) are fields defined on the Yee lattice. However, in contrast to the original FDTD method, the left-hand sides (LHSs) of these equations are a linear combination of fields at five points. Therefore, it is impossible to directly determine the values of fields at new times using these equations.

The LHSs of Eqs. (40) and (41) can be written symbolically as

$$\sum_{m,n} \sigma(x_0, y_0; x_0 + m\Delta x, y_0 + n\Delta y) B_z(t_0 + \Delta t, x_0 + m\Delta x, y_0 + n\Delta y, z_0), \tag{42}$$

$$\sum_{m,n} \sigma(x_1, z_1; x_1 + m\Delta x, y_1, z_1 + n\Delta z) D_y(t + \Delta t/2, x_1 + m\Delta x, y_1, z_1 + n\Delta z), \tag{43}$$

where

$$\sigma(\xi, \eta; \xi + m\Delta\xi, \eta + n\Delta\eta) = \frac{5}{6}\delta_{m,0}\delta_{n,0} + \frac{1}{24}(\delta_{m,1}\delta_{n,0} + \delta_{m,-1}\delta_{n,0} + \delta_{m,0}\delta_{n,1} + \delta_{m,0}\delta_{n,-1}), \tag{44}$$

and $\delta_{p,q}$ is the Kronecker delta defined as

$$\delta_{p,q} = \begin{cases} 1 & (p = q) \\ 0 & (p \neq q) \end{cases}. \tag{45}$$

The inverse operator "σ^{-1}" is defined as

$$\sum_{p,q} \sigma(\xi, \eta; \xi + p\Delta\xi, \eta + q\Delta\eta)\sigma^{-1}(\xi + p\Delta\xi, \eta + q\Delta\eta; \xi + m\Delta\xi, \eta + n\Delta\eta) = \delta_{m,0}\delta_{n,0}. \tag{46}$$

Using σ^{-1} enables Eq. (40) to be rewritten as

$$\begin{aligned}
&B_z(t_0 + \Delta t, x_0, y_0, z_0)\Delta x\Delta y = B_z(t_0, x_0, y_0, z_0)\Delta x\Delta y - \sum_{m,n} \sigma^{-1}(x_0, y_0; x_0 + m\Delta x, y_0 + n\Delta y) \\
&\times \Bigg\{ \frac{11}{12}\Bigg[\left(E_y\left(t_0 + \Delta t/2, x_0 + \left(m + \frac{1}{2}\right)\Delta x, y_0 + n\Delta y, z_0\right) - E_y\left(t_0 + \Delta t/2, x_0 + \left(m - \frac{1}{2}\right)\Delta x, y_0 + n\Delta y, z_0\right)\right)\Delta y \\
&- \left(E_y\left(t_0 + \Delta t/2, x_0 + m\Delta x, y_0 + \left(n + \frac{1}{2}\right)\Delta y, z_0\right) - E_y\left(t_0 + \Delta t/2, x_0 + m\Delta x, y_0 + \left(n - \frac{1}{2}\right)\Delta y, z_0\right)\right)\Delta x\Bigg] \\
&+ \frac{1}{24}\Bigg[\Bigg(E_y\left(t_0 + \Delta t/2, x_0 + \left(m + \frac{1}{2}\right)\Delta x, y_0 + (n+1)\Delta y, z_0\right) + E_y\left(t_0 + \Delta t/2, x_0 + \left(m + \frac{1}{2}\right)\Delta x, y_0 + (n-1)\Delta y, z_0\right) \\
&- E_y\left(t_0 + \Delta t/2, x_0 + \left(m - \frac{1}{2}\right)\Delta x, y_0 + (n+1)\Delta y, z_0\right) - E_y\left(t_0 + \Delta t/2, x_0 + \left(m - \frac{1}{2}\right)\Delta x, y_0 + (n-1)\Delta y, z_0\right)\Bigg)\Delta y \\
&- \Bigg(E_x\left(t_0 + \Delta t/2, x_0 + (m+1)\Delta x, y_0 + \left(n + \frac{1}{2}\right)\Delta y, z_0\right) + E_x\left(t_0 + \Delta t/2, x_0 + (m+1)\Delta x, y_0 + \left(n - \frac{1}{2}\right)\Delta y, z_0\right) \\
&- E_x\left(t_0 + \Delta t/2, x_0 + (m-1)\Delta x, y_0 + \left(n + \frac{1}{2}\right)\Delta y, z_0\right) - E_x\Big(t_0 + \Delta t/2, x_0 + (m-1)\Delta x, y_0 \\
&+ \left(n - \frac{1}{2}\right)\Delta y, z_0\Big)\Bigg)\Delta x\Bigg]\Delta t\Bigg\} + O(\Delta t)^3.
\end{aligned} \tag{47}$$

In addition, Eq. (40) can also be rewritten as

$$
\begin{aligned}
D_y(t_0+\Delta t/2, x_1, y_1, z_1)\Delta x\Delta z &= \left(D_y(t_0-\Delta t/2, x_1, y_1, z_1) + i_y(t_0, x_1, y_1, z_1)\right)\Delta x\Delta z \\
&\quad + \sum_{m,n} \sigma^{-1}(x_1, z_1; x_1+m\Delta x, z_1+n\Delta z) \\
&\times \left\{\frac{11}{12}\left[\left(H_x\left(t_0, x_1+m\Delta x, y_1, z_1+\left(n+\frac{1}{2}\right)\Delta z\right) - H_x\left(t_0, x_1+m\Delta x, y_1, z_1+\left(n-\frac{1}{2}\right)\Delta z\right)\right)\Delta x\right.\right. \\
&- \left.\left(H_z\left(t_0, x_1+\left(m+\frac{1}{2}\right)\Delta x, y_1, z_1+n\Delta z\right) - H_z\left(t_0, x_1+\left(m-\frac{1}{2}\right)\Delta x, y_1, z_1+n\Delta z\right)\right)\Delta z\right] \\
&+ \frac{1}{24}\left[\left(H_x\left(t_0, x_1+(m+1)\Delta x, y_1, z_1+\left(n+\frac{1}{2}\right)\Delta z\right) + H_x\left(t_0, x_1+(m-1)\Delta x, y_1, z_1+\left(n+\frac{1}{2}\right)\Delta z\right)\right.\right. \\
&- \left. H_x\left(t_0, x_1+(m+1)\Delta x, y_1, z_1+\left(n-\frac{1}{2}\right)\Delta z\right) - H_x\left(t_0, x_1+(m-1)\Delta x, y_1, z_1+\left(n-\frac{1}{2}\right)\Delta z\right)\right)\Delta x \\
&- \left(H_z\left(t_0, x_1+\left(m+\frac{1}{2}\right)\Delta x, y_1, z_1+(n+1)\Delta z\right) + H_z\left(t_0, x_1+\left(m+\frac{1}{2}\right)\Delta x, y_1, z_1+(n-1)\Delta z\right)\right. \\
&- \left.\left.\left. H_z\left(t_0, x_1+\left(m-\frac{1}{2}\right)\Delta x, y_1, z_1+(n+1)\Delta z\right) - H_z\left(t_0, x_1+\left(m-\frac{1}{2}\right)\Delta x, y_1, z_1+(n-1)\Delta z\right)\right)\Delta z\right]\right\}\Delta t \\
&+ O(\Delta t)^3.
\end{aligned} \tag{48}
$$

Then, the algorithm of the corrected FDTD method, which is supported by the next-to-the-lowest-order approximation, can be obtained by using Eqs. (48) and (47) repeatedly.

4. Numerical results

In this section, numerical results of electromagnetic wave transmission in a two-dimensional slab waveguide based on the original and corrected FDTD methods are compared with the analytical result.

Figure 3 shows the slab waveguide used in the computational methods, and **Figure 4** shows its calculation domain. This system consists of core and cladding

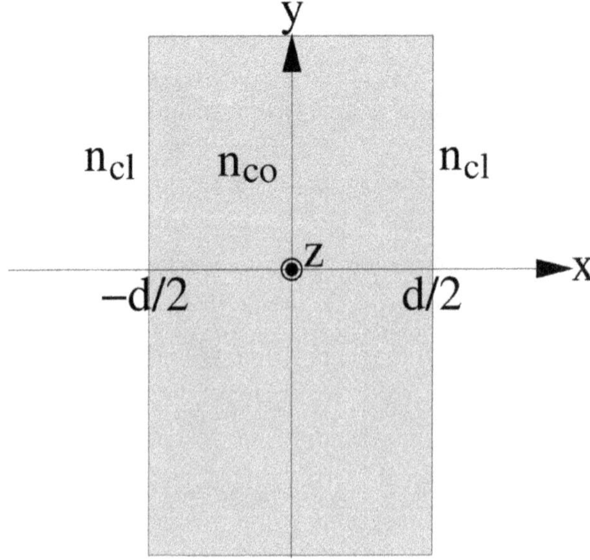

Figure 3.
Slab waveguide used in numerical calculation.

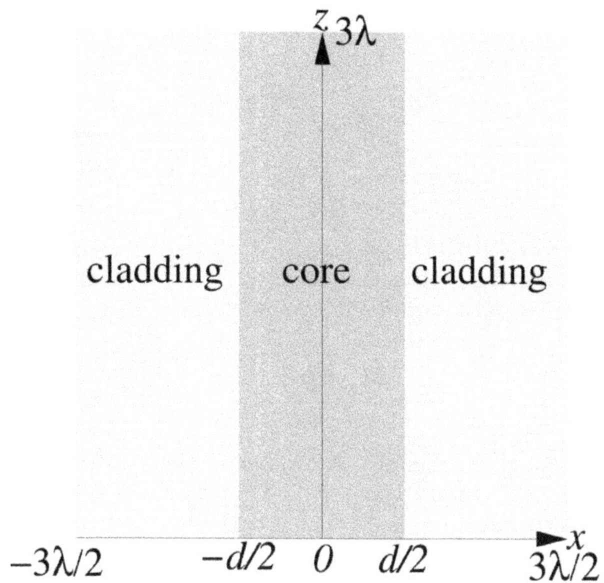

Figure 4.
Calculation domain.

regions whose indices are n_{co} and n_{cl}, respectively. The core region is extended infinitely in the y- and z-directions and has width d in the x-direction. The cladding region is the rest of space. An electromagnetic wave propagates in the z-direction, and its electromagnetic field is assumed to have no y dependence. Because the system has no y dependence, it is essentially a two-dimensional system. An analytical solution is known and is derived in the appendix. The solution is

$$E_x^{anl}(t,x,y,z) = \begin{cases} \dfrac{\beta h_0}{\omega n_{co}^2 \varepsilon_0} \cos\left(\dfrac{2ux}{d}\right) \sin\left(\omega t - \beta z\right) & |x| \le \dfrac{d}{2} \\ \dfrac{\beta h_0}{\omega n_{cl}^2 \varepsilon_0} \cos\left(u\right) e^{-\frac{w(2|x|-d)}{d}} \sin\left(\omega t - \beta z\right) & |x| > \dfrac{d}{2} \end{cases}, \tag{49}$$

$$E_y^{anl}(t,x,y,z) = 0, \tag{50}$$

$$E_z^{anl}(t,x,y,z) = \begin{cases} \dfrac{2uh_0}{\omega n_{co}^2 \varepsilon_0 d} \sin\left(\dfrac{2ux}{d}\right) \cos\left(\omega t - \beta z\right) & |x| \le \dfrac{d}{2} \\ \dfrac{2wh_0}{\omega n_{cl}^2 \varepsilon_0 d} \operatorname{sign}(x) \sin\left(u\right) e^{-w\frac{2|x|-d}{d}} \cos\left(\omega t - \beta z\right) & |x| > \dfrac{d}{2} \end{cases}, \tag{51}$$

$$H_x^{anl}(t,x,y,z) = 0, \tag{52}$$

$$H_y^{anl}(t,x,y,z) = \begin{cases} h_0 \cos\left(\dfrac{2ux}{d}\right) \sin\left(\omega t - \beta z\right) & |x| \le \dfrac{d}{2} \\ h_0 \cos\left(u\right) e^{-w\frac{(2|x|-d)}{d}} \sin\left(\omega t - \beta z\right) & |x| > \dfrac{d}{2} \end{cases}, \tag{53}$$

$$H_z^{anl}(t,x,y,z) = 0, \tag{54}$$

where "anl" indicates that this is an analytical solution. u and w satisfy

$$w = \left(\frac{n_{cl}}{n_{co}}\right)^2 u \tan(u), \tag{55}$$

$$v^2 = u^2 + w^2 = \frac{(n_{co}^2 - n_{cl}^2) d^2 \pi^2}{\lambda^2}, \tag{56}$$

where λ is the wavelength in a vacuum, ω is the angular frequency, and β is the propagation constant. The propagation constant is the propagation directional component of wave number vector and calculated as

$$\beta = \frac{2\pi\sqrt{n_{co}^2 w^2 + n_{cl}^2 u^2}}{v\lambda}. \tag{57}$$

v defined by Eq. (56) is called the V-parameter, which is determined by the parameters defining the system. u and w are determined using **Figure 5**. In the figure, red curves represent Eq. (55) which is symmetric under the parity transformation $x \mapsto -x$ as

$$H_y(t, -x, y, z) = H_y(t, x, y, z). \tag{58}$$

Brown curves represent

$$w = -\frac{n_{cl}^2}{n_{co}^2} u \cot(u), \tag{59}$$

which is antisymmetric under the parity transformations $x \mapsto -x$ as

$$H_y(t, -x, y, z) = -H_y(t, x, y, z). \tag{60}$$

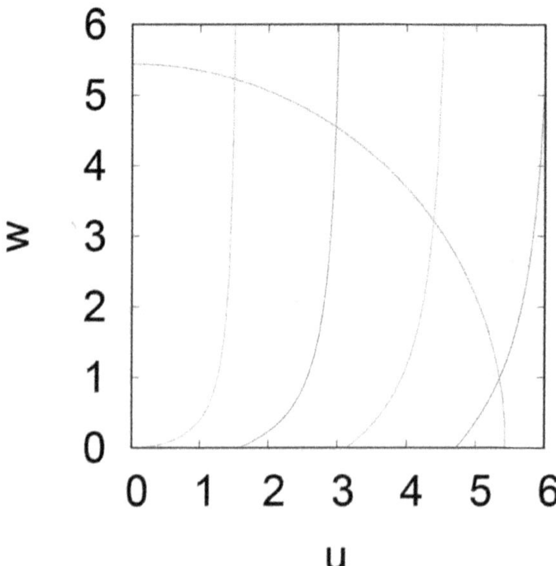

Figure 5.
Graphs of Eqs. (55), (59), and (56) to determine u and w.

The blue curve shows Eq. (56). At each intersection of curves Eqs. (55) and (56), there is an independent symmetric mode satisfying Eq. (58), and at each of the curves Eq. (59) and (56), there is an independent antisymmetric mode satisfying Eq. (60). The mode with the lowest u is called fundamental mode. The number of modes of the system is determined by V and increases by one with respect to each $\pi/2$.

In the computational methods, the system parameters are set with the wavelength λ as 0.30m, the core width d as 0.30m, the same with the wavelength, the core index n_{co} as 2.0, and the cladding index n_{cl} as 1.0. The lengths of the cell edges Δx and Δz are both $\lambda/20$, and the time step Δt is 10^{-12} s. With these parameter values, the parameter values of the analytical solution in Eqs. (49)–(54) can be derived as

$$u = 1.50, \tag{61}$$

$$w = 5.23, \tag{62}$$

$$v = 5.44, \tag{63}$$

$$\frac{\beta\lambda}{2\pi} = 1.94, \tag{64}$$

where the LHS of Eq. (64) is called the effective index, a value between n_{cl} and n_{co}. These parameter values show that the solution is the fundamental mode. A magnetic field is excited at $z = 0$ as

$$H_y(t, x, 0, 0) = \begin{cases} h_0 \cos\left(\frac{2ux}{d}\right) \sin(\omega t) & |x| \leq \frac{d}{2} \\ h_0 \text{sign}(x) \cos(u) e^{-\frac{w(2|x|-d)}{d}} \sin(\omega t) & |x| > \frac{d}{2} \end{cases}, \tag{65}$$

with the parameter values in Eqs. (61) and (62).

Figures 6–14 are numerical and analytical results at times at which the ωt values are integer multiples of 2π. In these figures, violet curves represent H_y/h_0, and green curves represent core and cladding regions. The region in which the value is 0.5 is the core region with index 2.0, and the region in which the value is -0.5 is the cladding region with index 1.0. In the figures, time goes downward. The time values are 1.0, 5.0, 10.0, and 20.0 ns. The left-hand column is calculated using the original

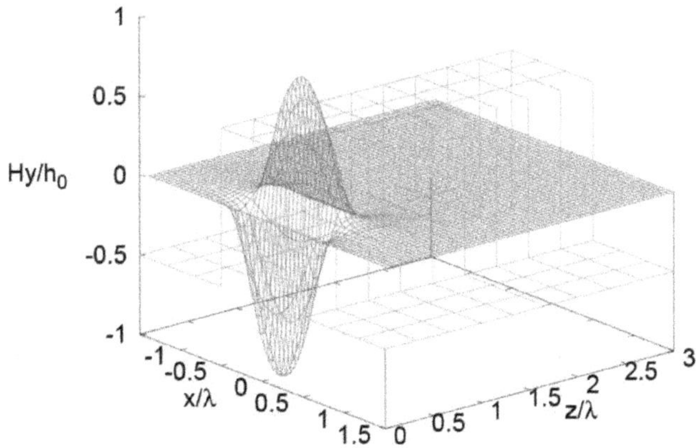

Figure 6.
H_y calculated using original FDTD method at $t = 1.0 \times 10^{-9}$ second.

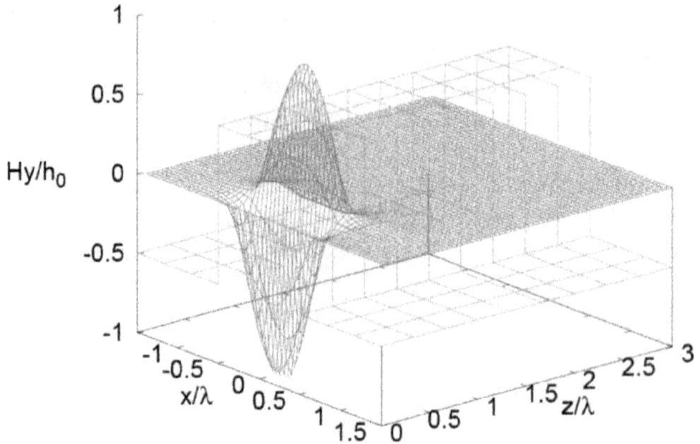

Figure 7.
H_y calculated using corrected FDTD method at $t = 1.0 \times 10^{-9}$ second.

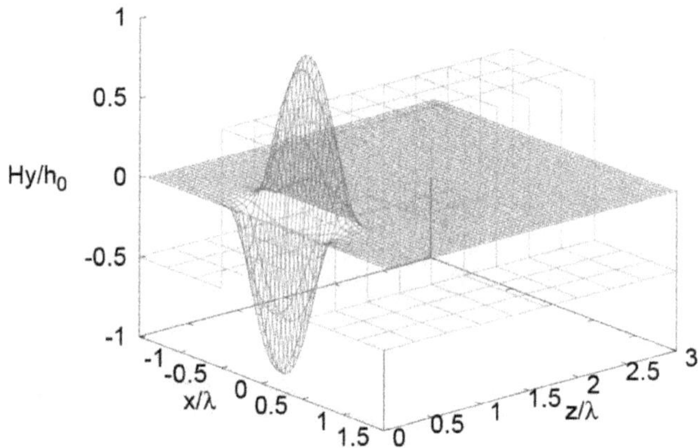

Figure 8.
H_y analytically calculated at $t = 1.0 \times 10^{-9}$ second.

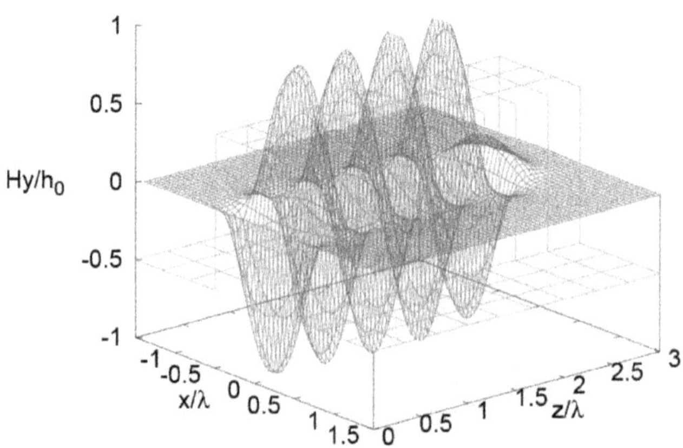

Figure 9.
H_y calculated using original FDTD method at $t = 5.0 \times 10^{-9}$ second.

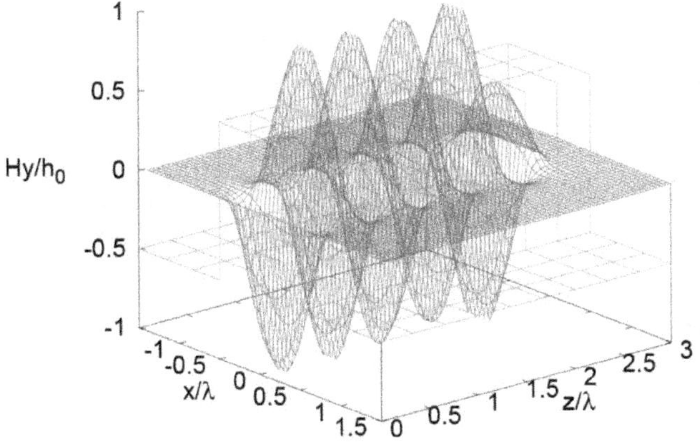

Figure 10.
H_y calculated using corrected FDTD method at $t = 5.0 \times 10^{-9}$ second.

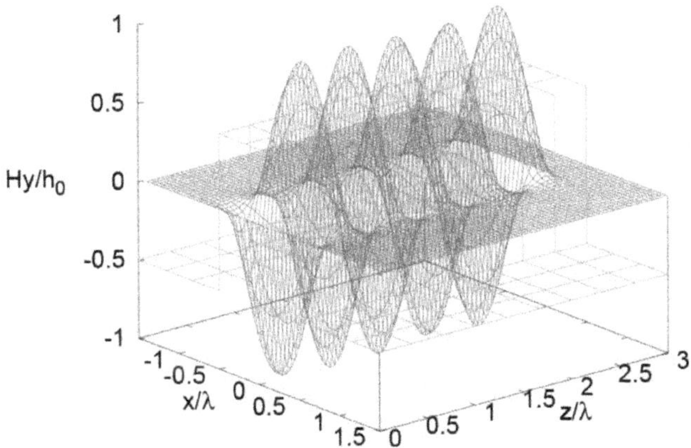

Figure 11.
H_y analytically calculated at $t = 5.0 \times 10^{-9}$ second.

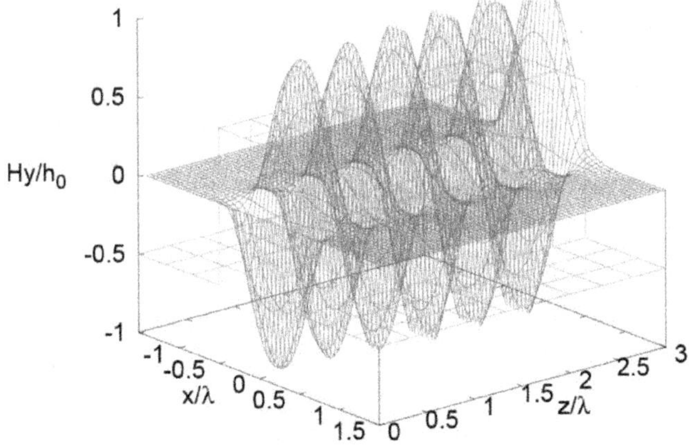

Figure 12.
H_y calculated using original FDTD method at $t = 1.0 \times 10^{-8}$ second.

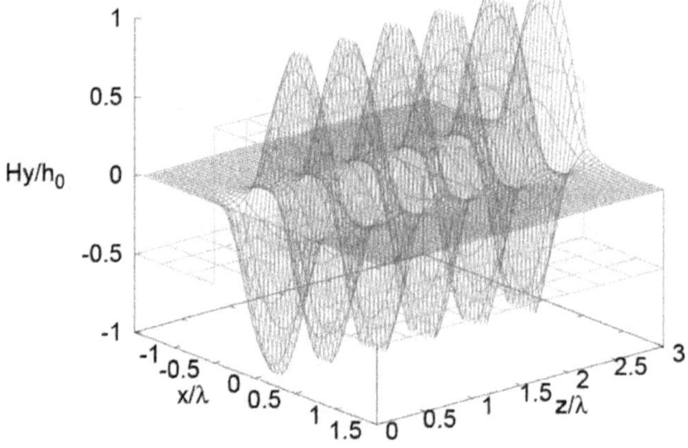

Figure 13.
H_y calculated using corrected FDTD method at $t = 1.0 \times 10^{-8}$ second.

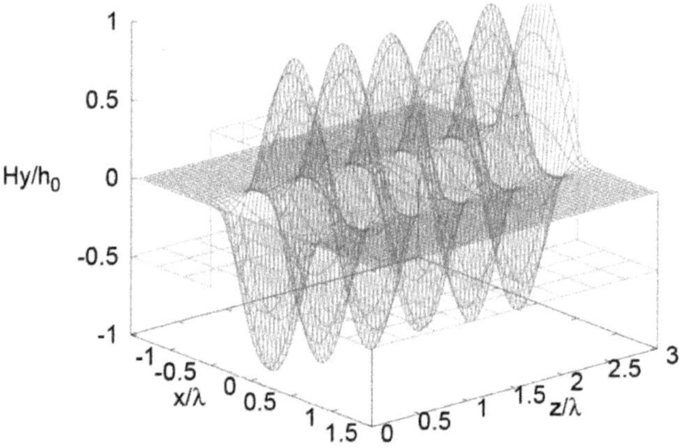

Figure 14.
H_y analytically calculated at $t = 1.0 \times 10^{-8}$ second.

FDTD method, the middle column is calculated using the corrected FDTD method, and the right-hand column is the analytical solution wherein the region

$$\omega t < \beta z, \tag{66}$$

H_z is zero. Moreover, the differences in the results between the FDTD calculations and those of the analytical ones make it clear that $|H_y/h_0|$ at some points exceeds one in the FDTD calculations, even though the values at any point are equal to or less than 1 in the analytical results. However, the differences in the calculation results between the original and corrected FDTD methods are unclear. This indicates that it is impossible to conclude whether the corrected FDTD method is better than the original one using these figures.

To compare the accuracy and reliability of the original and corrected FDTD methods, we use a function $err(t)$ defined as

$$err(t) = \frac{\sum_{p,q} \frac{H_y^{num}(t,p\Delta x,0,q\Delta z) - H_y^{anl}(t,p\Delta x,0,q\Delta z)}{n(p\Delta x,0,q\Delta z)^2}}{\sum_{p,q} \frac{H_y^{anl}(t,p\Delta x,0,q\Delta z)^2}{n(p\Delta x,0,q\Delta z)^2}}, \tag{67}$$

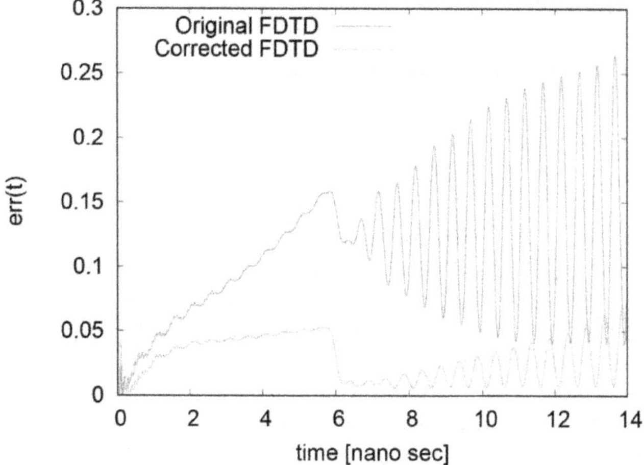

Figure 15.
$err(t)$ of the original and corrected FDTD methods.

which shows the error between the FDTD and the analytical calculations at each time. In Eq. (67), the denominator of the right-hand side is proportional to the power of the propagating electromagnetic wave passing through the $x - y$ plane per unit length of the y-direction.

Figure 15 shows the *err* functions of the original and corrected FDTD methods defined by Eq. (67). As shown in the figure, almost every time except for less than 0.14 ns, the *err* function of the corrected FDTD method is less than that of the original. This means that the corrected method is more accurate than that of the original. In addition, when the time is greater than 6 ns, both curves begin to oscillate. The amplitude of the oscillation of the corrected FDTD method is clearly less than that of the original. This indicates that the corrected method is more reliable.

5. Conclusion

In this chapter, a higher-order correction to the original FDTD method supported by the next-to-the-lowest-order approximation of the integral form of Maxwell's equation was shown. The essence of this method is the approximation of integrals over a cell surface and edge using discretized electric and magnetic fields.

The results of numerical calculations of an electromagnetic wave propagating in a two-dimensional slab waveguide using the corrected and original FDTD methods and analysis were also shown. The differences between the corrected and original FDTD methods were compared using the *err* function, and the corrected method was found to be more accurate and reliable than the original.

Acknowledgements

The author would like to thank Mr. A. Okabe, who is the collaborator of reference [2], which is based on this chapter. The author would also like to thank Enago (www.enago.com) for the English language review.

Conflict of interest

The author declares no conflicts of interest associated with this manuscript.

A. Appendix

A.1 Analytical results of two-dimensional slab waveguide

The analytic solution of an electromagnetic wave in a slab waveguide shown in **Figure 3** is provided in various textbooks regarding optical waveguides and related fields [5–8]. In this appendix, the analytical results of Eqs. (49)–(54) are derived in accordance with these references.

A propagating electromagnetic wave with no y-dependence in the z-direction with angular frequency ω and propagation constant β, the wave number in the z-direction, is written as

$$\boldsymbol{E}(t,x,y,z) = \boldsymbol{e}(x)e^{i(\omega t-\beta z)}, \tag{68}$$

$$\boldsymbol{H}(t,x,y,z) = \boldsymbol{h}(x)e^{i(\omega t-\beta z)}. \tag{69}$$

Maxwell's equations in dielectrics using Eqs. (13) and (22) become

$$i\mu_0\omega h_x(x) = -i\beta e_y(x) \tag{70}$$

$$i\mu_0\omega h_y(x) = i\beta e_x(x) + \partial_x e_z(x), \tag{71}$$

$$i\mu_0\omega h_z(x) = -\partial_x e_y(x), \tag{72}$$

$$in(x)^2\varepsilon_0\omega e_x(x) = i\beta h_y(x), \tag{73}$$

$$in(x)^2\varepsilon_0\omega e_y(x) = -i\beta h_x(x) - \partial_x h_z(x), \tag{74}$$

$$in(x)^2\varepsilon_0\omega e_z(x) = \partial_x h_y(x), \tag{75}$$

where $n(x)$ is the index distribution shown in **Figure 16**. As shown in Eqs. (70)–(75), there are two closed equation classes. The first class contains Eqs. (70), (72), and (74), which have components of electric and magnetic fields transverse to the propagation direction and a longitudinal component of the magnetic field in that direction. The second class contains Eqs. (71), (73), and (75), which have components of electric and magnetic fields transversed to the propagation direction and a longitudinal component of the electric field in that direction. Solution to the first class comprise the transverse electric (TE) mode because the electric field has only a component transversed to the propagation direction, and solution to the second class comprises the transverse magnetic (TM) mode because the magnetic field has only a component transversed to that direction. In Section 4, numerical and analytical results of H_y are shown, and they are TM modes.

Hereafter, our discussion is limited to the TM mode. Then, Eqs. (71), (73), and (75) are rewritten as

$$\partial_x^2 h_y(x) = -\left[\left(\frac{2\pi n(x)}{\lambda}\right)^2 - \beta^2\right] h_y(x), \tag{76}$$

$$e_x(x) = \frac{\beta}{n(x)^2\varepsilon_0\omega} h_y(x), \tag{77}$$

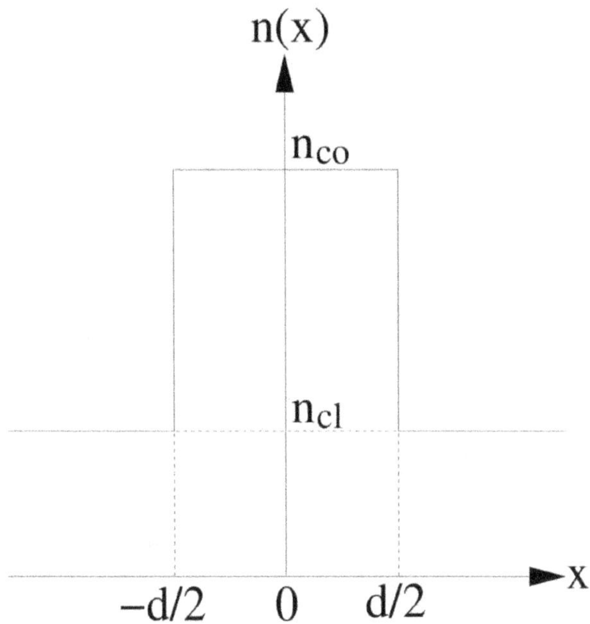

Figure 16.
Index distribution of the slab waveguide.

$$e_z(x) = \frac{1}{in(x)^2\varepsilon_0\omega}\partial_x h_y(x). \tag{78}$$

The discontinuity of $n(x)$ at $x = -d/2$ and $x = d/2$, shown in **Figure 16**, requires that the boundary condition at $x = \pm d/2$ be considered. Because of the integral form of Maxwell's equations, the components of electric and magnetic fields parallel to the boundary surface of the indices are continuous, and the components of the electric and magnetic flux densities normal to the surface are continuous. Consequently, $H_y(x)$ and $\partial_x h_y(x)$ in Eqs. (76)–(78) are continuous.

Solving Eq. (76) requires considering the following three cases:

1. $|\beta| < n_{cl}$
2. $n_{cl} \leq |\beta| < n_{co}$
3. $n_{co} \leq |\beta|$

In case 1, the solutions of Eq. (76) are

$$h_y(x) = \begin{cases} Q\cos(Px) & (|x| \leq d/2) \\ \left[\begin{array}{l} \left[Q\cos\left(\frac{Pd}{2}\right)\cos\left(\frac{Qd}{2}\right) + P\sin\left(\frac{Pd}{2}\right)\sin\left(\frac{Qd}{2}\right)\right]\cos(Qx) \\ -\left[P\sin\left(\frac{Pd}{2}\right)\cos\left(\frac{Qd}{2}\right) - Q\cos\left(\frac{Pd}{2}\right)\sin\left(\frac{Qd}{2}\right)\right]\sin(Qx) \end{array}\right] & (|x| \geq d/2) \end{cases}, \tag{79}$$

and

$$h_y(x) = \begin{cases} Q\sin(Px) & (|x| \le d/2) \\ \left[\begin{array}{l} \operatorname{sign}(x)\left\{ \left[Q\sin\left(\frac{Pd}{2}\right)\cos\left(\frac{Qd}{2}\right) - P\cos\left(\frac{Pd}{2}\right)\sin\left(\frac{Qd}{2}\right) \right]\cos(Qx) \right. \\ \left. + \left[P\cos\left(\frac{Pd}{2}\right)\cos\left(\frac{Qd}{2}\right) + Q\sin\left(\frac{Pd}{2}\right)\sin\left(\frac{Qd}{2}\right) \right]\sin(Qx) \right\} \end{array} \right] & (|x| \ge d/2), \end{cases} \tag{80}$$

where

$$P = \sqrt{\left(\frac{2\pi n_{co}}{\lambda}\right)^2 - \beta^2}, \tag{81}$$

$$Q = \sqrt{\left(\frac{2\pi n_{cl}}{\lambda}\right)^2 - \beta^2}. \tag{82}$$

However, this solution does not show electromagnetic wave propagation in the z-direction but shows a reflection and transmission problem of the film when the incident angle is less than the critical angle. Let us discuss this in more detail. When $|x| \le d/2$, $H_y(t,x,y,z)$ is a linear combination of

$$e^{i(\omega t - Px - \beta z)}, \quad \text{and} \quad e^{i(\omega t + Px - \beta z)}, \tag{83}$$

a plane wave whose wavenumber is $(P, 0, \beta)$ and $(-P, 0, \beta)$, respectively. When $|x| > d/2$, $H_y(t,x,y.z)$ is a linear combination of

$$e^{i(\omega t - Qx - \beta z)}, \quad \text{and} \quad e^{i(\omega t + Qx - \beta z)}, \tag{84}$$

a plane wave whose wavenumbers are $(Q, 0, \beta)$ and $(-Q, 0, \beta)$, respectively. Therefore, with a suitable linear combination of Eqs. (79) and (80), the solution becomes that a plane wave with wavenumber $(P, 0, \beta)$ is incident from the $x < -d/2$ region to be reflected and transmitted by a film of the $|x| \le d/2$ region with a reflected wave propagated in the $x < -d/2$ region and a transmitted wave propagated in the $x > d/2$ region. Therefore, this solution is not what we want.

In case 2, the solutions of Eq. (76) are

$$h_y(x) = \begin{cases} \cos(Px) & |x| \le d/2 \\ \cos\left(\frac{Pd}{2}\right) e^{-Q\frac{2|x|-d}{d}} & \end{cases}, \tag{85}$$

where

$$P = \sqrt{\left(\frac{2\pi n_{co}}{\lambda}\right)^2 - \beta^2}, \tag{86}$$

$$Q = \sqrt{\beta^2 - \left(\frac{2\pi n_{cl}}{\lambda}\right)^2}, \tag{87}$$

$$\frac{Qd}{2} = \left(\frac{n_{cl}}{n_{co}}\right)^2 \frac{Pd}{2} \tan\left(\frac{Pd}{2}\right), \tag{88}$$

and

$$h_y(x) = \begin{cases} \sin(Px) & |x| \leq d/2 \\ \text{sign}(x)\sin\left(\frac{Pd}{2}\right)e^{-Q\frac{2|x|-d}{d}} & |x| > d/2 \end{cases}, \tag{89}$$

where

$$\frac{Qd}{2} = -\left(\frac{n_{cl}}{n_c o}\right)^2 \frac{Pd}{2}\cot\left(\frac{Pd}{2}\right). \tag{90}$$

Defining

$$u = \frac{Pd}{2}, \tag{91}$$

$$w = \frac{Qd}{2}, \tag{92}$$

yields Eqs. (53), (55), (56), and (59). This is the solution we want.
In case 3, the solutions of Eq. (76) are

$$h_y(x) = \begin{cases} \cosh(Px) & |x| \leq d/2 \\ \cosh\left(\frac{Pd}{2}\right)e^{-Q(|x|-d/2)} & |x| > d/2 \end{cases}, \tag{93}$$

where

$$P = \sqrt{\beta^2 - \left(\frac{2\pi n_{co}}{\lambda}\right)^2}, \tag{94}$$

$$Q = \sqrt{\beta^2 - \left(\frac{2\pi n_{cl}}{\lambda}\right)^2}, \tag{95}$$

$$Q = P\tanh\left(\frac{Pd}{2}\right), \tag{96}$$

and

$$h_y(x) = \begin{cases} \sinh(Px) & |x| \leq d/2 \\ \text{sign}(x)\sinh\left(\frac{Pd}{2}\right)e^{-Q(|x|-d/2)} & |x| > d/2 \end{cases}, \tag{97}$$

where

$$Q = -P\coth\left(\frac{Pd}{2}\right). \tag{98}$$

As a result of Eqs. (94) and (95),

$$-P^2 + Q^2 = \left(\frac{2\pi n_{co}}{\lambda}\right)^2 - \left(\frac{2\pi n_{cl}}{\lambda}\right)^2, \tag{99}$$

is satisfied. When P is pure imaginary and Q is real, the solution reduces to case 2. There is a possibility that Q is neither real nor purely imaginary. However, such a solution must be attenuated when z becomes large. Mathematically, there can be a divergent solution when z becomes large, but such a solution cannot conserve energy. Therefore, such a solution is not what we want.

Author details

Naofumi Kitsunezaki
Amashiro Science, Nagoya, Japan

*Address all correspondence to: n.kitsunezaki@amashiro-science.jp

References

[1] Yee K. Numerical solution of initial boundary value problems involving Maxwell's equations in isotropic media. IEEE Transactions on Antennas and Propagation. 1966;**14**:302-307. DOI: 10.1109/TAP.1966.1138693

[2] Kitsunezaki N, Okabe A. Higher-order correction to the FDTD method based on the integral form of Maxwell's equations. Computer Physics Communications. 2014;**185**:1582-1588. DOI: 10.1016/j.cpc.2014.02.022

[3] Kitsunezaki N. Higher-order Correction to the Finite-Difference Time-Domain Method Based on the Integral Form of Maxwell's Equations. In: BIT's 4th Annual Global Congress of Knowledge Economy; 19–21 September 2017; Qingdao, Dalian: BIT Group Global Ltd.; 2017. p. 096

[4] Nielsen HN, Ninomiya M. A no-go theorem for regularizing chiral fermions. Physics Letters. 1981;**B105**: 219-223. DOI: 10.1016/0370-2693(81) 91026-1

[5] Marcuse D. Light Transmission Optics. 2nd ed. New York: Van Nostrand Reinhold Company Inc; 1982. 534 p. ISBN: 0-442-26309-0

[6] Haus HA. Waves and Fields in Optoelectronics. Prentice Hall: Englewood Criffs; 1983. 402 p. ISBN: 0-139-460-535

[7] Buch JA. Fundamentals of Optical Fibers. Hoboken: Wiley; 2004. 332 p. ISBN: 0-471-221-910

[8] Okamoto K. Fundamentals of Optical Waveguides. San Diego: Academic Press; 2006. 561 p. ISBN: 0-12-525096-7

www.ingramcontent.com/pod-product-compliance
Lightning Source LLC
Chambersburg PA
CBHW081234190326
41458CB00016B/5775
* 9 7 8 1 8 3 8 8 0 6 5 8 3 *